MW00817163

ABOVE AND BEYOND

How a tall, lanky kid from the Omaha Housing projects spent
a lifetime helping others top their dreams

Dr. Rodney Wead
As told to Dr. Ann Wead Kimbrough

AWVB PUBLISHING

ATLANTA, GEORGIA

AWVB Publishing
4129 Pepperdine Drive
Decatur, Georgia 30034

Ordering Information: Quantity sales. Special discounts are available on quantity purchases by corporations, associations, and others. For details, contact the publisher at the address above.

Cover Design by Veverly Byrd-Davis

Above and Beyond/ Dr. Rodney Wead. -- 1st ed.
ISBN 978-1-7371937-0-8

"What I appreciate most is Rodney's lifelong dedication
to the empowerment of his people and his
undying love of helping others."

— CATHY LIGGINS HUGHES

Founder and Chairperson of Urban One Media Company

In one of the most challenging years of the century, Rodney's story of perseverance, strategy, and tremendous opportunity is right on time. When I heard Rodney Wead was working on his biography, I was thrilled -- even more, I was honored when he asked me to write the foreword. The title of the book, "Above And Beyond," seems almost serendipitous. As soon as I read the rough draft, I knew this story was one for the books. This man has got more moves than Allied Van Lines! Rodney knows that people don't do what you say, they do what they see you doing! So, he's been busy doing the darn thing! He demonstrates how tremendous opportunity, friends, and mentors can inspire every "man, woman, and child" to overcome their limitations and fulfill their purpose on earth. The Most High has blessed Rodney, and to know him is a gift.

In this book, you will discover how one person gained the power to transcend prejudice and change the landscape for black and white communities across the country. You will uncover just how vital relationships can be in providing growth, fulfillment, and the many moments of happiness needed to persevere against all odds. With roots sprouted in Omaha, Nebraska, he didn't just fight for civil rights; he fought for human rights.

Rodney Wead is a real-life superhero, but we all know great things take a village. In the pages that follow, you'll meet his superhero friends. People like Cathy Hughes, the first African American woman to head a publicly traded corporation. And Bob Boozer, a gold medal Olympian and 1971 NBA Championship winner with the Milwaukee Bucks. You'll also meet Bob Gibson (endearingly known as "Gibson"), Hall of Fame Pitcher with the St. Louis Cardinals and

Charles B. Washington, a journalist, mentor, and civil rights activist who stayed loyal to the cause until the day he died.

The true measure of a (wo)man is their ability to get back up. In "Above and Beyond," you will realize that perseverance is a direct pathway to fulfillment. Rodney is a survivor; he's gone to hell and back. All of us can find a piece of ourselves in that story, especially in times when many of us are fiercely searching for happiness. I believe that happiness comes from surviving struggle, challenge, and failure. You will read how Rodney's darkest moments lead him to his highest points of personal growth, self-knowledge, and fulfillment. Most importantly, in reading this book, I hope you discover that accomplishing true happiness through service to others is only half of the battle. The real key is balance -- we must courageously commit to the service of our authentic selves.

"Above and Beyond" is a manifesto -- an ethos of resilience and a timeless embodiment of purpose and strength. So, I say emphatically, Rodney and those who have known Rodney have lived full, enriching lives, and I am pleased to call him my friend and mentor. His story is proof that many of the greats throw themselves into the mess -- put themselves on the line, stare adversity right in the face, and dream big. That's what our friend Cathy did; it's what Gibson did, Gayle did, and heck, I'm going to go for it too! How about you? After all, we were just some kids from Omaha.

Every Day is Game Day.

Johnny "The Jet" Rodgers
1972 Heisman Trophy Winner and
Husker Player of the Century

FOREWARD

....

This work shines the light on the path that far too many Americans of African descent have been forced to follow to achieve a piece of the American Dream. Separated from our ancestors by the violence perpetrated against us that is woven into the fabric of this nation. Migrating in search of better opportunities for ourselves and our families. Working the jobs that the color of our skin allowed us to fill, e.g., the packing houses and the railroads. And, believing that obtaining a good education would make a difference in our lives. By shining this light, the author, my dear friend and mentor, Rodney Wead, reveals the many parallels in our lives, although nearly separated by a generation.

My parents, like Rodney's, migrated to Omaha in search of better jobs. My father worked in the packing houses although he, like Rodney did much later, had attended Langston University for one year. My father purchased our first home on Pinkney Street. My parents placed an extremely high value on education and, as a result, they sent me to Omaha Central High School although I, like Rodney, really wanted to attend Omaha Technical High School with many of my friends. I share Rodney's delight in the fact that our parents made that decision.

Not only are there numerous parallels surrounding my life and Rodney's life, but his work also intersected at various junctures with my own work. Rodney shared his athletic gifts by coaching the neighborhood softball team. While acknowledging that I was as good, if not better, than the boys on his team, he would not allow me to play because I was a girl. I did not think it was fair that I was not allowed to play, but I didn't harbor any ill will towards Rodney. However, when I got older and more confident, I began referring to Rodney as my first "male chauvinist pig."

As Rodney poured himself into community building, I was both an indirect and direct beneficiary of his efforts. Because of his involvement in the purchase of KOWH AM and FM, I and my high school classmates were able to groove to soul music in our homes and in our cars. The degree I earned from the University of Nebraska-Lincoln was due in large part to the scholarship funded by the late Susan "Susie" Buffett and was administered by Rodney through the Wesley House Community Center.

Rodney's commitment to his community created opportunities for me to be of service. Little did either of us know that I would ultimately become Chairwoman of the Board of the Community Bank of Nebraska, the Black-owned bank founded by a group led by Rodney. I was also one of the members of the African American community that Rodney brought together with members of the Jewish community to form the Black/Jewish Dialogue.

Although Rodney has spent the last several years sharing his gifts and talents in the St. Louis area, his presence is still felt in Omaha. In fact, we are reminded of him every time we drive or walk down "Rodney S. Wead Street.," which was dedicated in his honor in 2018. The publication of this work is a testament to the fire that still burns within him. Thank You Dr. Rodney S. Wead!

With Love,
Brenda J. Council
Former Nebraska State Sen. (D-11)
Mayor" of Pinkney Street

ACKNOWLEDGEMENTS

To name every person who has touched my life would likely double the pages of this book.

In no way would I wish to offend anyone by unintentionally leaving them out of my acknowledgements for commendable presence in my life.

I believe that the contents of this book will honor everyone with deep appreciation either through their names, experiences, times-and-places, memories of loved ones and other references. Thank you for allowing me to present the parts of my life that I have remembered. If I left something out of my recounting of a long and grateful life, count it to my head and not my heart.

-- Rodney S. Wead, Ph.D.

CONTENTS

PART ONE

CHAPTER ONE

Living Just Above Water

In 1935, the year that I was born in Omaha, Nebraska, "it was the best of times, it was the worst of times, it was the age of wisdom." It was 1859 when Charles Dickens penned those words to contrast good and evil in A Tale of Two Cities. His description of London and Paris was apropos for the 1930s Omaha of black and white communities where Dickens-like "the spring of hope ... winter of despair" was evident.

Omaha's population was about 200,000 with approximately 10 percent African Americans, or "colored people" as we were called then, when I came onto this planet. My Dad, Sampson Luster Wead, was born with the surname Weed and was born second from the youngest to a proud family of educators and merchants in Helena, Arkansas, a once vibrant city at the Mississippi River in the Delta Region of the deep South. Dad changed the spelling of our last name to "Wead" from "Weed" in part out of fear that the mob who killed his father in the 1919 "race riots" would be looking for Weeds in addition to all black men. His mother Cora Weed (later Wead) somehow shepherded her tall, brawny sons and handsome daughters out of Arkansas in late 1919 or early 1920. Her husband, my grandfather, was killed by white mobs. While we cannot locate specific records, my grandfather, William Weed, was among a group of black men seeking to raise money to pay the legal fees for poor black farmers seeking fair wages from their cotton field landowners. The great Ida B. Wells-Barnett came to the Helena and Elaine, Arkansas area to bravely report for the NAACP's Crisis magazine about the black men, including my grandfather, who withstood unfair justice in the courtroom and bloodied streets where dogs and gunshots tore apart bodies. So much of our family legacy was lost during those days in September 1919.

My father carried those tragic memories with him to his grave. Such gaps in not knowing more about my mother and father and their families were things we shrugged off.

Although I cannot tell you how and why I knew, there was just a kind of secret society among black people of a certain age. My experience is typical of most blacks as our history is often lost or stolen.

I do know that my father and mother met in Omaha. My mother, Daisy Shanks Wead, was born in the beautiful Florida Gulf Coast city of Pensacola. My mom along with her mother; my grandmother, Ann Brayboy Green, arrived in Omaha in 1928. My parents, who met in Omaha, were among the estimated 6 million blacks who made up the Great Northward Migration beginning in 1916. They sought better lives that included jobs, social and educational improvements.

My Mom and Dad married and briefly left Omaha for Minneapolis, Minnesota. There they set up shop as store owners. They returned to Omaha by 1930. My Dad joined the Meat Cutters Local No. 33 as he lugged heavy sides of beef during the early years of his lifetime career at Cudahy Packing Company in South Omaha. I was the second child from my Mom's bosom. The first one was my sister, Barbara, who died in infancy. We were stairstep children -- born one year apart from each other. My sister, Beverly, was next to me and my brother Sam was the youngest. We had a lot of fun during those depression-era years. Our Christmases were full of toys, gifts, and festivities until it came to an abrupt stop one year.

We were very fortunate to initially enjoy a modest and comfortable life as renters of a two-story home in a mixed-raced neighborhood in North Omaha. Mom and Dad also sublet a couple of the rooms in our homes, a custom of many in our neighborhood because it was during WWII and it was difficult for people to afford decent housing. We had a big kitchen and nice-sized bedrooms. The neighborhood was known as Little Pensacola. Most of the new Pensacola residents were located where I was born which was between 24th and Grant Street north to 30th and Patrick Street. Ninety percent of the occupants of the one- and two-story homes were black people.

CHAPTER TWO

The Good and the Bad with my Dad

I was proud of my Dad. He was a powerful man of 6'2 ½, and about 210 pounds with a solid build. He was considered one of the best beef lugers in the meatpacking industry. Dad was making good money and I recall the shiny 1936 Pontiac he bought. That is when I started loving Pontiacs and still do so today.

As much as I looked up to my Dad, there were things he did to bring me down. He would physically fight with my mother. During those times, my brother, sister, and I would hug one another to drown out the grownups' fights. One day around 1942, we all had an earth-shaking experience. It was when my Dad walked out on my mother and us. Sadly, my mother did not have many marketable skills.

I have never forgotten what it feels like to live in such poor conditions. With Mom and Dad divorced and Dad out of the house, we had no income. I remember that he allotted Mom ten bucks a week. I will never forget how important that ten bucks was to our minimal survival. Oftentimes, my Dad would skip weeks of pay to Mom, and that was awfully hard for us. Besides my wonderful mother, my dynamic grandmother was our guardian angel. The sun rose and set on my mother from my grandmother's standpoint. We felt loved.

DePorres Club members, including Rodney Wead's father (front left), protest Reed's Ice Cream in 1953 for not hiring blacks.

Sampson Luster Wead was rarely photographed. That is what makes this photo so special.

Source: Unknown

My mother and grandmother did housework for white folks in Omaha's Benson area. My grandmother, Ann Green or "Gram" as we called her, earned pretty good money. Mom was busy raising us, so her former housework jobs were mostly put on hold. We fell into a hole so deep, that we could barely get out of it.

With all the doom in my young life, there was a big highlight of 1940. It was the memory of my mother holding my hand and walking me to Lake School for the first day of kindergarten. It was one exciting moment in my life. My new school was a ten-minute walk from our house. My Mom's best friend, who also was named Daisy, accompanied us. I remember meeting my first teachers, Ms. Olson, and Ms. Deidrick. They were so kind to me. It was a mixed-race school. Besides the black students, there were a lot of Russians, Jews and Germans attending Lake School.

The day came when the owner of the house that we lived in found a renter who could make timely, monthly payments. We had no choice, but to move. We moved in with my grandmother in 1944 in a tough neighborhood at 20th and Burdette Streets. It was riddled with crime and the area was labeled as the slums with run-down, three-story houses that were divided to make apartments. The apartments were only two- and three-rooms. We lived on the third floor and we shared our bathroom with one apartment dweller who lived on the other side of the house. Our apartment was airy. We did not have a kitchen or sink. We did have an icebox to store our food.

The landlord, Mr. John Robinson, had a strict rule: No children allowed. But my grandmother was more concerned about us having a place to live. She was tough. Occasionally, she would flash her little revolver and that was apparently enough to keep the landlord away. Our neighbors also looked out for us. They would warn us with "Mr. Robinson's coming." My grandmother would always calmly say, "Come on kids. We must hide." That was fun to hide from the landlord. All the while, I believed that he knew we were living there. I also believed he was afraid of my petite, and feisty grandmother. I have a good story to share about her in a later chapter.

Mom and Gram converted the large living room into a bedroom and my sister, brother and I slept in a smaller bedroom. Inside our apartment, we had a pot stove in the area where my mother and grandmother slept. It was also our family's gathering spot at night. My brother, sister, and I got fuel for the pot stove by gathering wood and leftover coal along the nearby train tracks.

The bathroom was located outside of the apartment, so it was exposed to no heat or no air conditioning. The bathroom was freezing during the Nebraska winters. My Mom came to the rescue with a portable heater that we could take with us to the bathroom. It was quite an event for my family to take turns with the neighbors on the other side of the house to go to this awful looking bathroom. In the summer months, it was very hot in our apartment and the bathroom. It was suffocating in the bathroom and we learned how to hold our breaths when going in and out of the bathroom.

Daily, I was reminded that indeed we were impoverished. Very few people lived as poor as we did for that one year, 1944-45. Fortunately, we attended a very decent school, Lake School.

I grew up fast and at age 9, I began to hang out with some rough guys. Thankfully, as the Lord would have it, I got a part-time job as a delivery boy at a local grocery store, Houston Grocery. The owner built a bike for me with an oversized delivery basket. I worked after school and all-day Saturday. I made $5 a week. Man did that money come in handy for our family. I was able to purchase our groceries at a much cheaper rate at Houston Grocery and I gave my mom $2 a week. She allowed me to keep $3. I shared my earnings with my brother and sister and often, we spent part of our money watching movies at the old Ritz Theatre.

During the worst of times, we made the best of our situation as a poor family. One day, Mom announced the good news that we were moving to the Logan Fontenelle Housing Projects that were built in the late 1930s as part of President Franklin Roosevelt's New Deal's Public Works Administration. When a father or the primary breadwinner moves out of the house, the household suffers. Our prayers were answered.

Our playground at Logan Fontenelle Housing Projects.
Courtesy of the Farm Security Administration – Office of War Information Photograph
Collection (Library of Congress).

CHAPTER THREE

Moving on Up

The landlord from our first home, Dr. Lennox, recognized my Mom's name on a long waiting list for available public housing units. Fortunately, he moved up our application for housing after my mother pleaded our case. Moving to the low-income Logan Fontenelle Housing Projects was like moving from a hole in the wall to a mansion.

Logan Fontenelle Housing Projects forever changed my life. It consisted of 250 units, each with two or three bedrooms. The racial mix was evenly divided; there were 125 residences for Negroes on the east side and 125 units for Caucasians on the west side.

Kellom Elementary School children at the end of our school day in 1945.

Source: Omaha Public School System

It was a far cry from our life in Gram's place. We never owned a refrigerator and my siblings, and I thought it was a piece of furniture! My sister, Beverly, and I used to open the refrigerator and stick our heads inside the freezer because it felt like air conditioning. Once our mother caught us, that was the end of our curiosity with the cool air.

My siblings and I joined a wonderful new school, Kellom Elementary School. The school was racially integrated and comprised of economically poor students. Later, I learned that famed actor and dancer, Fred Astaire attended Kellom. The school also became known for other famous alumni including my best buddy and St. Louis Cardinals Cy Young Award winner, Bob Gibson. Former Omaha mayors and more celebrities attended Kellom. I am convinced that because I was born during such a time filled with progressive New Deal programs, established, and implemented between 1933 and 1942, that it was embedded in me to appreciate and advance housing programs for the poor, seek financial reforms for the disenfranchised, employment and educational attainment. Much like President Franklin D. Roosevelt who proclaimed during his first inaugural address, "let me assert my firm belief that the only thing we have to fear is fear itself," I've lived what some described as a fearless life and one that is blessed.

CHAPTER FOUR

Foundational Friendship

I gained the whole world in my new home. I was blessed to gain three sets of brothers with one set becoming two of my best friends. The first set were Bob and David Gibson. Their big brother, Josh, introduced me to Bob and David. They were the first dudes whom I met on the playground at Kellom Elementary School. Bob and I were in the fifth grade. Little did I know that Bob would become a professional baseball Hall of Famer. Bob, David, and I had the best times playing sports during those precious days in our youth. The Gibson brothers were gifted with great hands, minds, and athleticism. They were excellent in all sports and in arts and crafts.

Isaiah and Herbie Davis, another set of brothers, equally were as proficient in sports. Isaiah was a brilliant mathematician. He was awarded a scholarship to Iowa State University. Isaiah had a stellar career where he helped design one of the first space capsules at Cape Canaveral in Florida. Herbie became the first black battalion chief of the Omaha Fire Department.

The third set of brothers were Norman and Leonard Hudgens. Norman became a foremost karate expert and one of the best judges within the sport. He was nationally ranked within the U.S. Air Force.

His brother, Leonard, became a boxing great and earned a Golden Gloves Boxing championship.

My other best friend was Willie Mills. He was one of the first blacks in the country to operate a computer mainframe at Creighton University, one of a handful of elite colleges to be awarded federal grants for computer research. During Willie's senior year at Creighton, he brought me to a large room on the campus and showed me a machine that was the same size as the room. He graduated with honors and worked on some of the first computers during the 1950s and 1960s.

Besides my male friends, I had great female friends, including Beverly Essex (now Shoba). I considered her my other sister and she happened to be my sister Beverly's best friend.

I began to call my best buddy "Gibson" instead of Bob. We used to sit on the curb in front of 24th and Charles streets and compete for who could name the most interesting guys cars.

We also were dazzled by the men who would "konk" their hair. "Konk" was a process where lye was placed in the hair and turned kinky hair into "white hair." Gibson and I would often remark about "good hair" or another name for white people's hair. When my mother caught us, she told us that our hair was "good hair" and never to negatively compare anything about ourselves to other people again.

Gibson and I would also hide in the bushes and watch the streetcars travel one way down Lake Street and turn around. There were gambling joints along 24th Street, crap shooting was big and there were plenty of houses of ill repute. We were exposed to just about everything – good and bad – in our youth and yet we were able to stay clear of the law and pursue our education. The riskiest chance I took was with my other buddy, Herbie.

Herbie and I decided that we were going to steal some comic books. We put a comic book inside of another comic book and would walk out. We knew that we got away with it after we left the store and headed back to Herbie's church, a Seventh-day Adventist Church (SDA) at 27th and Lake Street. That is, until we saw our Moms waiting for us. We knew something was different because our Moms never came out of the house at night. They gave us a couple of good hits upside our heads that hurt more afterward than before because my friends made fun of me for 20 years. We found out later that Rev. Ernest Graham, pastor of the Church of the Living God, told our parents what we did.

We had a great time growing up under the watchful and teaching leadership of Gibson's big brother, Josh. Josh returned home from military service with a college degree from a fine school, Tuskegee College (now University) and yet, he was unable to find a job in the teaching field. Josh was a great man with tremendous skills and experience. He was not discouraged. Josh organized our youth baseball team and named it the Y Monarchs in 1948 patterned after one of the best Negro League teams, the Kansas City Monarchs. He also honored the YMCA with the name.

I credit Josh for inspiring me to become a student-athlete who valued academics as much as athletics. While we played baseball at the old Burdette Park, Josh was working on earning his master's degree at Creighton University. He rode his bike between Creighton and the Burdette Park baseball field, and he always had his schoolbooks with him. When he placed his books on the bench, I was always curious about what he was reading. Often, I peeked inside of his books. One day I asked Josh what kind of information was inside his books. He talked to me about school and the importance of going to both high school and college. Importantly, Josh sparked my interest in studying history by telling me to read certain books with historical perspectives.

Josh also had a master plan that was carried out with a lot of hard work on his part and that also came with hateful rejection and huge odds against his success. It was clear that he built our team around Gibson's skills. We did not mind. Josh began with recruiting the best athletes in the projects. He carried a stopwatch to time our speed. We were all fast runners, good ball handlers and excellent batters. Since we won so many games around Omaha, Josh decided we should cross the Missouri River and play against guys in the small, mostly white Iowa towns known as Woodbine, Avoca, Hamburger and Iowa City. From 1949 – 50, we were considered the best team in the Midwest.

Baseball was a cherished sport during this time and in those communities. It was a new stadium in Woodbine, Iowa and we opened it up against 14 and 16-year-olds just like us. Gibson hit a line drive over the left field fence, and we were in awe because we had never seen anyone hit a homerun in person before then. Neither did anyone in the park expect a person that young to hit a ball that far in the field. He was quite an athlete.

We played and won a lot of games in Iowa. After the games in Iowa, they always fed us watermelons. I loved watermelons and I think Gibson did as well. But Gibson never liked to eat watermelon in front of the other teams, so he would duck out and go back to the bus and eat his watermelon. He did not like how the people looked at us eating it. Gibson said they took pictures of us as we ate the watermelon. Gibson was always observant about the inequities in society.

What I knew about Gibson is that he feared no one. He was fierce. The only person who I remember Gibson being afraid of was some big guy when we were in grade school. His name was Donald Moore. Anyone who we feared, we always called them by their first and last names. One of those times when Gibson and I were going to the restroom, Donald Moore told Gibson that he was going to beat him up. Gibson turned to me and said that Donald Moore said he was going to beat us up.

Gibson and I had great speed and were always confident to outrun anyone who would chase us. That day at lunch, Gibson and I sprinted down the street, but we had to stop running to obey the safety patrol girls. One was Gibson's sister, Barbara Jean. She asked why we were running and we told her that Donald Moore was chasing us. She said that she would take care of that. Kellom Elementary School did not have a cafeteria. Barbara Jean then allowed us to cross 22nd Street to go home and have lunch. By the time we returned from lunch and back to school, we had forgotten about the confrontation. We were walking to the restroom again when we saw Donald Moore. Gibson said, "Here comes Donald Moore. Donald Moore walked up to us and said, "Hi fellas. How are you doing? Have a good day." We knew that Barbara Jean had taken matters into her own hands.

That story stuck with me as we grew older. In 1949-50, we were winning in baseball. When we came back to segregated Omaha, we were denied the opportunity to play in the American Legion Baseball league. But we were able to get into the playoffs against the league in Columbus, Ohio. We won the Nebraska State championships, the first black team to do so. We were excited to say the least.

Our next adventure came when Josh accepted the invitation for our team to travel to Kansas City and St. Joseph, Missouri to play the best black ballplayers in our age range. We were so excited because it also meant that we would stay in our first hotel room. Josh did not have the heart to tell us that we would not play simply because we were Negroes. We traveled those hundreds of miles only to find out that we had to sleep on pool tables at the local YMCAs. Nevertheless, we had a great time laughing at Gibson's cut ups. We had a great time sleeping on the Y's pool tables.

We emerged as winners in more ways than one. It was a victory for all that we had to endure as a black team competing in a sea of white ballplayers.

The winning Y Monarchs in 1948. I am seated second in the center; Gibson is fourth on the right line.

Source: The Wead Collection

CHAPTER FIVE

GLORY YEARS

The Kansas City Monarchs in 1940s

Source: NLBM.com

The most pleasant memories of living in the projects were experiencing recreational activities. Softball was one very popular sport in Omaha. My buddy, Bob Gibson, Elwood Grant, Haskell Lee, and Herbert Davis could hardly wait for a Sunday during the summer months. We would change clothes from our "Sunday best," and journey from our neighborhood to the Burdette field about a mile away from home during those 1945, 1946 and 1947 summers.

Upon arrival to the historic Burdette Field, we would gaze upon our superheroes in softball. They were the great W.O. Brooks, "Ace"

Hill softball pitchers and Ed Brooks, a sure handed third baseman; and all were All-American.

When the great W.O. would arrive, my buddies and I would elbow our way as far as we could to watch W.O. dress for the big game. He would carefully tie his cleats and polish his baseball shoes. He would joke with his teammates and start warming up his fabulous right arm. The umpire would say, "play ball!"

The tall, handsome dark-skinned brother was called up to the pitcher's mound. My buddies and I would be frozen in ecstasy. We would watch W.O. make the first pitch. He would pause to get the sign from the catcher. Then the catcher would say, our other superhero, would say, "bring it." He would wind up in marvelous motion and make a very fast pitch to the plate. What an experience to witness a seven-inning game and watch our superheroes!

CHAPTER SIX

My Tough Granny
-vs- The Hood

*Homes in North Omaha in my neighborhood in the
1930s – 1940s.*

Source: Omaha.com

Baseball was not the only outside activity to occupy my life. I also had a paper route. Ever since I began working at age nine as a delivery boy at a local grocery store, I worked for the rest of my years. Even now in retirement, I am sometimes called upon to teach a college course or two. As a youngster, I worked to help support my mother, brother, and sister. It was instilled in me at an early age that my work was valuable to my family.

I was proud to be the first person in my family to progress as high as the eighth grade. I remember my Omaha World-Herald daily newspaper paper route. Having won two of its three Pulitzer Prizes in the 1940s for its exemplary coverage, the newspaper was considered pretty good. Carl Palmquist was the manager of the paper routes and he had a team of 30 young guys who delivered the Omaha World-Herald all over the northside of Omaha. We had to turn in our money to Mr. Palmquist and we kept a hefty share of it. I think it was 10 or 15 bucks.

My paper route on 23rd and Grace and Clark streets were in the red-light district. On one side of the street were the houses of ill repute. I would get to go inside because I was carrying the paper. I learned a lot by watching those prostitutes as a 13- and 14-year-old boy. It just so happened that one day I was being distracted by something that took place and someone took my satchel that was attached to my belt. My mother made the satchel for me to carry my money. It was a tough neighborhood, and the people were not always honest about paying 25 cents a week for the newspaper. I would place extra quarters in my satchel because too often, if someone gave me a dollar and I gave them 75 cents, they would accuse me of not giving them the right amount. It was easier for me to give them the extra quarter than to argue with them.

I delivered newspapers on Friday evenings and was fortunate to be able to listen to a popular radio disc jockey named Harry Best. He was a black man who was my favorite announcer at a Council Bluffs, Iowa radio station. He played soul music; the good stuff that my mother also exposed me to. The music would waft from the windows along my paper route and it made my job so delightful. In those days, the type of music that Harry Best of KSWI Radio played was called "race music." It was sort of forbidden to be heard by blacks. That was the rhythm and blues era before rock and roll became popular. I was 13 years old and it was the beginning of an idea that I one day wanted to have my own radio station and hire Harry Best.

Omaha was a typical racist city. While the city promoted so-called integration, at its core it was racist and that is the reason Harry Best had to leave Omaha and travel far across the bridge and broadcast his two-hour show from Iowa. I remembered Harry Best when we established Omaha's and the nation's first black-owned AM and FM radio station, KOWH, 23 years later.

One day, all my money was in my satchel because I was going to turn the money into Mr. Palmquist and in turn receive my profit. I planned to go to the Ritz Theatre with my buddies – Gibson, the Davis brothers and my brother, Sam. I was heartbroken that I could not go to the movies with them because I did not have any money. I was also embarrassed that someone stole it from me, and I had to tell my mother what happened.

My Mom was passive and laid back and avoided serious arguments. But my grandmother was a terror and when she found out about it, she came to our place with the sword that was entombed in a cane. She wanted me to show her where it was stolen. I had to walk past my buddies who made fun of me because my small in stature -- 5-foot-tall -- grandmother was going to get back my satchel for her towering, 5'11" grandson.

Once we got to the densely populated apartments, my grandmother took her cane and knocked on many doors and challenged people to fist fights if they did not return my satchel. She was tough. Somehow my satchel appeared and with all my money in it! When I told my buddies what my grandmother had done, they had incredible respect for her going into a tough neighborhood and coming out victorious.

CHAPTER SEVEN

The Reluctant "Chosen One"

My dear Mom was simply a wonderful mother. I would not have made it past the eighth grade if it were not for her tender, loving care, and her concern about my wellbeing. She made every rite of passage for me an exciting one. I was the first in the family to graduate from grade school and boy, did she make it a big deal. I was really feeling good about myself. I got my first suit, a blue one, and my first new pair of Tom McCann shoes. My Uncle John bought them for me. Uncle John knew that Mom was struggling, and he always went out of his way to do something for Mom. Our dear Uncle John was always ready to help us. He was a great pianist and when he learned that my sister Beverly wanted to play the piano, he got one for her and moved it into a very small space in the projects. Can you imagine? It took up half the room where we used to be able to sit down. But it was great because we had this grand gift to remind us that we were loved. Mom made it clear that she wanted all her kids to do what she did not do, which was graduate from grade school and high school.

I just knew that I would attend Omaha Technical High School because all my buddies were going there. But that was not in the cards because Dr. Edith Hall, principal at Kellom Elementary School, got to my mother and strongly suggested that I attend the city's premier college preparatory high school. My Mom told me that I would attend

Omaha Central High School in the fall, and I was down for a few months about her decision.

It turned out that Central High was the greatest decision my Mom made for me. My life turned around and changed for the better, again. I traveled to school by taking the 24th and Lake Street streetcar with two girls, who also became my dear friends. Dorcas Mills, Beverly Essex and I were the only three Negroes to attend Central High while all of our friends were having a great time attending Tech High. Years later, we often reminisced about our time at Central High and we all agreed that we were happy with the decisions for us to attend and graduate in four years from the college preparatory school.

The Central High building was an impressive structure that was over a 100- years-old and located on a hill overlooking downtown Omaha. It was once the site of Nebraska's first capitol building before the capitol city was changed to Lincoln. The three-story building was built in a square with an open courtyard in the center of the school. When I attended, each of the four sides had two sets of stairs and the boys' and girls' restrooms were on the landings. When walking with a girl, you had to separate as the boys were not allowed on the girls landing and vice versa. The school did not have air conditioning. Even my kids who also attended Central High, had to endure what I endured.

As a new student at Central High, I tried out for three sports and earned athletic letters in all. I also joined the Army ROTC, but quickly dropped that extracurricular activity. As a freshman who was nearly 6'4," I was easily the tallest person on the basketball court. I played some pretty good ball during my high school years and received lots of media coverage. The coursework was tough, yet I loved history and poetry and did well in those subjects. I had a rough time academically my first year, but I studied harder in my sophomore and subsequent years at Central High and my grades improved.

The second year, I was better. During my sophomore year, I had the most traumatic experience in my young life. I was pretty cocky, and I prepared to try out for the football team. I thought that I had avoided that freshman hazing ritual known as "canning." It was when guys were thrown in trash cans. I was talking mess in the Room 235 study hall when one of the guys threatened to throw me in the can. I snapped back, "You can't throw me in the can. I am a sophomore." It took four senior football players to pick me up and throw me in the trash can. It was so embarrassing. They broke my left shoulder.

As I tried to crawl out of the trash can, the first people who I saw were Annette Davis and Angeline Owen. Little did I know that Angeline would be my future wife. Those two ladies were a sophomore and a freshman and the horrified looks in their eyes quickly let me know that I was in bad shape. They were able to get me up and I got medical treatment. The doctor put my shoulder in a cast, and I missed the entire football season.

> But I was happy to make the varsity football team a year later. Later, in my 20s and 30s, some of the guys would tease me, "Hey Wead, we canned you at Central High School."

"Canning" was a rite of passage for us athletes and it made for good stories years later. My junior and senior years were outstanding. Behind me now was that terrible "canning" incident. I began to grow up more. I was having more fun at home. I did not date much. I was too busy with sports and the jobs that I had to do to help my family.

I could not afford too much anyway. In the spring of 1952, Omaha had a major flood along the Missouri River. A high-water mark was predicted that would top all the levies that protected both Omaha and Council Bluffs. The cities were basically shut down. All the cities' available equipment and workers were mobilized at the river to fill sandbags and build temporary dikes. That lasted for more than one week. My good friends, Gibson and I worked on the river for long days and nights – only seeing each other briefly at home. When the danger was over, we got together and compared our experiences. Gibson said he volunteered only because his older brother Josh made him do so. Hudgins and I signed up for work through a construction company and received union wages for our efforts.

Even though Gibson and I lived only one block apart, we never saw much of each other during those four years. He was at Tech High, busy with his activities, and I was at Central High with my activities. We acquired new friends, but we would always touch base occasionally. David, his brother, and I became even closer friends and we loved going down to the corner store, listen to records made by great artists and share a hamburger.

My junior year was my best year as an athlete at Central High and was the first time I thought about college. I did well in football, basketball, and track. I was always fast and became quite a sprinter during those years and that ability would follow me through my college career. My junior year was also a pivotal point for me as far as my future education. Gibson's brother Josh also encouraged me to pursue a higher education. Thank God my Mom was able to get us into the housing projects because I was friends with fellas who also wanted to go to college or pursue other careers after high school.

PART TWO

CHAPTER EIGHT

Staying Alive

Dana's Weed wins 100 . . . as Omaha U's Olson (left), Sterba and Hardy trail.

Winning ways were common for me at Dana College.

Source: Omaha World-Herald Photos

With my glorious high school days behind me, I looked ahead to college. Gibson and I went different routes after high school. He was such a natural athlete and was a strong competitor in all categories of sports. He earned a basketball scholarship at Creighton University, yet he still loved baseball. Gibson was wise to play both sports at Creighton.

Meanwhile, I was recruited to play basketball at Langston University in Guthrie, Oklahoma by the famous Caesar Felton "Zip" Gayles. He was one of the greatest coaches of black institutions at that time. He came to Omaha and recruited me. I was excited as I got ready to go to Langston in 1953. My Dad accompanied me on the train to Guthrie, Oklahoma and we said our good-byes to friends and family who remained in Omaha. There were too many to count.

My Mom packed our lunches in shoeboxes, which was the common way Negroes carried our food since we could not eat in the same areas as whites. Many of my white friends from Central High were on that same train and were going to Oklahoma University. We laughed and talked until the first train stop.

My Dad and I were directed to another train car in Kansas City, Missouri. Now sitting in a smelly section of the train that included cattle; I was mortified and instead of looking forward to the start of my college days, I rode the rest of the way to Oklahoma mostly silent. When the train whistle signaled that we had arrived, my Dad and I trekked to Langston. I was not prepared for the shock of being that far away from home. I was homesick. Without that much counseling and guidance, I packed up my belongings and made it back home to Omaha, much to the surprise and disappointment of my Mom. Some of my friends teased me about coming back home.

An ex-coach, Ken Kennedy, heard of my plight. He spoke to a high school rival coach from Dana College, Paul Peterson, who remembered me as a standout athlete in track, basketball, and football at Central High. Coach Peterson went above and beyond to get me enrolled at Dana in nearby Blair, Nebraska. I was the second black person admitted to Dana, despite my low college entrance exam scores.

I rode the bus to Blair, Nebraska and began to fend for myself. I had no idea where it was located, and some people asked me if I were lost. When I told them that I was entering Dana, they pointed up the hill. I had to walk those 10 miles to Dana and boy, that was something. I was assigned a room that I shared with Bud Kruse and we got along very well. Even though I qualified to play every sport at Dana, I could not get an athletic scholarship. To pay my tuition and fees, I scrubbed pots and pans in the school's cafeteria.

The cross on the hill behind the two dormitories, erected during the school year of 1949-1950, has always traditionally stood at the highest point of the campus.

Source: Dana College Archives

Dana College was a fine school, with an enrollment of around 500 students. It was a Scandinavian-sponsored school, and a majority of the student population were from the Danes and Swedes heritage. It was a highly regarded school with some of the finest Danish professors. Despite a perfect set up – friendly campus life, a non-bigoted roommate, and good students, I had a rocky first two years at Dana.

With Angeline no longer in my life and having to learn how to meet other people being a challenge for me, it was a very tough time in my life. I remained very active on the campus of Dana; we won a lot of games and had great celebrations. My buddy, Marion Hudson was already dating a white girl named Carol Larson. It was during this time that I became involved with a college sophomore, Elsie Lund, and we became intimate. One day, she told me that she was pregnant. I was quite surprised and quite anxious about this situation. Elsie just disappeared. I later found out that she moved back to Maine, had the baby and placed him up for adoption at the Lutheran Family Services of Nebraska in Omaha.

My situation with Elsie did not go away. Dana College president, Dr. Norton, found out that I had fathered a child with a white lady which had set him on kicking me out of school. His reaction stunned me, and it set me back emotionally. I was so worried. For an entire semester during my sophomore year, I endured humiliation and isolation. I was locked in a room for several days. It was 1955 and all I could think of was the horrible torture and lynching of 14-year-old black, Emmett Till in Mississippi. He was accused of disrespecting a white woman. I had a lot to think about and I was full of fear. I thought I was going to die.

As for me, as the Lord would have it, the Dean of Men, Dr. Frank Thomson, came to my rescue. I confessed to him what had happened. He was very, very sympathetic because he said that I was a decent student that did not cause any problems. He went down the road of misery and uncertainty with me; yet it was Dean Thomson who prevailed, and I was able to continue my studies.

As for the baby, several decades later I learned that he was adopted in Omaha by a fine family, and they named him Marc Vaughn. Ironically, I knew his adopted mother and father because they were great bowlers and occasionally, we bowled together. I knew nothing of their son and his relationship to me. It was years later that Elsie took the initiative to trace Marc and later found me. I reflected when my mother and grandmother learned of baby Marc. My Mom insisted that she wash and iron my clothes that I brought home often from college. Yes, she spoiled me a lot.

One day while watching Elvis Presley on our brand-new TV in the housing projects, I heard this loud yell coming from the upstairs apartment. I forgot that Elsie Lund had supplied me pictures of Marc when he was born, and I forgot I had left them in my satchel. I confessed to my mother that I was the father of the baby and I had no idea where the baby was. I resolved everything in my head by telling my Mom that Elsie disappeared and I never saw her again. That was indeed the Gospel truth. So, Mom and Gram sat me down at age 20 and talked to me about the birds and bees (chuckle). It was a little bit late for that and I told them that it will never happen again.

I learned that Marc also attended Central High and graduated from the University of Nebraska-Lincoln. He has a nice family and a successful career. He is doing quite well and we remain in close contact with one another. He also was immediately embraced by my then adult children; Candy, Gene, Nieve and Missy.

At Dana College, I learned my lessons and really concentrated on my studies after being released from on-campus solidarity existence. I regained my confidence that I would graduate from college. I was beginning to see pay dirt. I was so lucky in my junior and senior years to have some of the finest professors in the country.

Dr. Henry Swanson, or "Swanny" as we called him, was well-respected among historians across the globe and he encouraged me to excel in that specialized study.

Also, Dr. CC Madden was a wonderful theology professor and his influence helped me improve my grades. I became quite proud that I was now earning a bachelor's degree from Dana.

My junior and senior years went by at lightning speed. During the summer before my junior year, I was employed for the city and I worked for a gentleman named Lonnie Wilks. He took good care of me. I was getting behind in my payments to school and earning that bit of money lifted a big worry off my shoulders.

Dana was a private, Danish Lutheran school, and it was quite expensive. I was trying very hard to keep up with the tuition and fees and my studies.

Thankfully, that summer of 1956, Lonnie found a lot of work to keep me busy in the Omaha street and sewer departments. It was interesting work. Besides me, Lonnie hired two more college guys and we called him "Uncle Lonnie" while not knowing that one day, he would indeed become my uncle through marriage.

We worked in the sewer, and we chased and killed thousands of rats through the poison we would administer. They were big, well-fed rats from the Missouri River. Even though I did not like to deal with the creatures, I became used to them. I had big boots, and was very thin and athletic, so I could get in those manholes with no problem while fending off rats and killing as many as possible.

Lonnie was an interesting man. He loved his gin. Maybe that is why he passed so early in his life. He also had a lady friend who would fix him big sandwiches for lunch. But we knew that if he got a little taste of gin, then he would not eat his lunch. We would wait around like vultures watching him and see what he was going to do with his delicious lunch. Sometimes he would eat a little bit of lunch and often ask us if we wanted the remains of his lunch.

Uncle Lonnie was quite a guy and I really appreciate him for giving me extra work to get me through college. The highlight of my years at Dana College began with my acceptance into Kappa Alpha Psi Fraternity, Inc., Alpha Eta chapter.

I had excellent role models such as the first black principal in the Omaha Public School District, Dr. Eugene Skinner. My lifelong buddies, Isaiah Davis and John Lindsey and I were pledged for nine months. Isaiah and John were my fraternity line brothers and they have passed on, yet they each contributed greatly to our society's progress. Isaiah was a great mathematician and an inventor who worked at NASA. John became a pharmacist, and he perfected many techniques in his profession.

I am so blessed to have become a Kappa in 1955. I can still see my buddies and me in our blue suits and red ties when we were inducted at the John Butler YMCA in North Omaha. I am very proud of the fraternity and proud of my work in the fraternity. Today, I am even more proud as my grandson became a Kappa and so did many of my younger relatives.

Another highlight of my Dana years was graduating from college. I became the first in my family to earn a bachelor's degree. I was still living at home and commuting to Dana during my freshman year. I was fully an on-campus student during my sophomore year. My sister was preparing to enter her freshman year at the University of Nebraska Omaha and my brother was beginning to finish his senior year of high school. I was so proud to know that although my mother and grandmother had limited education, they encouraged us to complete high school and enter college. Those two did a great job.

Me and the brothers of Alpha Eta Chapter,
Kappa Alpha Psi Fraternity, Inc.

Source: The Wead Collection

I was absolutely convinced that many doors would now become open to me. I would become a teacher and proudly lead a great life with my family. Little did I know that the struggle ahead of me would be foreboding.

CHAPTER NINE

Harsh Realities

During my last days in college, I reunited with my high school girlfriend, Angeline Cecil Owen. We married on Sept. 8,1957. I never realized that the next year would be so challenging.

We moved into a triplex at 24th and Evans streets. Those old brick homes were not converted to modern day times. We had to order coal to get the furnace burning in the winter months. It was cold in the winter and hot in the summer. What made things worse was the obvious racism that hit me in the face. The so-called American dream was a nightmare for a college-educated black man seeking a decent job. People were laughing at my situation. I was so down in my spirit. If you were black and female, the jobs were available in the primary schools.

I hustled and found several odd jobs at a paper company and loading garbage. On some of the odd jobs that I worked, I took my oldest daughter, Candy, with me. She loved it and that would cheer me up as I continued to look for a full-time job that paid me a salary to support my family. I had no car and no job and my son, Gene, was sickly.

We really struggled. Angeline worked so hard at her job at Offutt Air Force Base, which was several miles away from our home in North Omaha. Angeline was pregnant with our middle child, Nieve, and that added to my pressure to achieve rightful employment.

In February 1958, I got the break I had been praying for when I was hired as an educational therapist teaching autistic and schizophrenic boys at the Nebraska Psychiatric Institute. I was so happy to get a job. I remember telling Angeline that we were on our way and indeed we were.

On the day that my daughter, Ann Lineve, was born on April 26, 1958, I held her in my arms and had an overall good feeling that things were going to get better. They did. To this day, I have never looked back or regressed. It was always onward and upward. I celebrate all of my kid's birthday, yet that day was the beginning of my career that would bring pride and joy to Omaha and to the Wead name.

Before long, I bought a nice car, a 1951 Pontiac and became very active in my church. It was Angeline's grandmother, Edna Robinson, who was my advocate at our church, Clair United Methodist Church (Clair UMC.) I became a Sunday School teacher, served on several committees, and was dedicated to attending services with my family. With a new job and some sense of security, Angeline and I were able to save enough money to buy a house for our family at 2437 Pinkney Street.

CHAPTER TEN

Pinkney Street

Me and my championship guys.

Source: The Wead Collection

This classic photo was taken after our strong victory to win the Panama, Iowa softball tournament on Sept. 4, 1960. There were 18 teams of boys, ages 12 – 13-years-old. We were the only black team in competition. Our team captain, Jerry Bartee, pictured in the center on the bottom row and on one knee, thankfully helped me remember the names of the great bunch of guys who created so many indelible memories. They are: Top row, left to right: Robbie Glover, Warren Willis, Michael McGinnis, Ronnie Bartee, me, Ricky Trimble, Allen Anderson, Paul Shannon, Gary Jamison and Willard Baker. Bottom row, left to right: Jack Childs (equipment manager.), Greg Butler, Jesse Jerry Bartee, Howard Duncan and Ed Morrow, nicknamed Bozo.

There were so many memorable times during that fantastic weekend in Panama, Iowa; yet leading up to the weekend tournament, I was terribly sick and confined to bed. I could tell that the boys were nervous and believed that we may not make the tournament because they hung around my house and kept asking about how I felt. I could hear Jerry, Ronnie and Willis practicing their catching and throwing in our front yard. I believe hearing them practice helped me to get better along with Mrs. Robinson's special medicine that she delivered to me.

We wanted to take the boys to Iowa in a van or a large bus, but the money was not there. Instead, the three of us drove the team. Our three-car caravan consisted of my good buddies, Tommy Davis, next door neighbor, Ryland Washington and me. Our cars were packed. Thanks to Angeline's grandmother, Mrs. Robinson, we received a donation of $50 from Clair UMC to pay for gas and any small expenses for the Iowa tournament. We were treated very well by the people in Panama, Iowa. Every boy on the 17 other teams were all decked out in crisp team uniforms. My guys wore their street clothes and a few with somewhat matching shirts. We simply could not afford nice uniforms.

In the final game, one of our outfielders, Howard Duncan, was our game hero by hitting two home runs. During the tournament, all the boys were playing at the top of their games. After we defeated the final team, we posed for our picture and drove back to Omaha, awaiting our trophy. It was a tall and glistening trophy and we shared it with our church family. They rewarded us – with Mrs. Robinson leading the charge – by purchasing new uniforms for us to play in during our third year the next summer.

Among the boys who stood out for his softball skills and off the field, was Jerry Bartee. Jerry was wise and his leadership abilities really helped me with team organization.

"I broke my glasses just before going to Iowa," said Jerry. "I had what they used to call 'Coke bottle' glasses. I borrowed my cousin, Carolyn's cat glasses and played in them."

Jerry also said that one of the highlights of winning that tournament and all of the games in Omaha during that summer season, was the food that awaited them. Angeline made and served sandwiches along with cookies, popsicles and Kool-Aid. Jerry and I remember what a treat that was for the team.

I will always remember this impressive group of boys. So many of them became outstanding leaders in their respective careers.

While preparing for the final season, Willis' younger sister, Brenda, appeared at the spring tryouts and demanded to play ball with the boys. I am embarrassed to admit that I responded to her in keeping with those times. I told Brenda that girls did not play softball with the boys. She was crushed and probably because she was such an asset to our team because she kept me abreast of the activities in our neighborhood but was only allowed to help as the "ball girl."

Yet, it was Brenda who helped me think differently. I had daughters and they would want to strive for more things that were then traditionally "male." Brenda was indeed a great athlete; she was feisty and a great orator. So much so that at her young age, she gave me a piece of her mind. She remained mad at me for a few years, yet Brenda became one of my trusted friends. Brenda had a resilience and an ear to the ground that was unlike any other young social and political activist in Omaha – at that time and perhaps through today.

Brenda also stood out in academics and her career goals. She earned the second scholarship awarded to promising black students from the Susan Thompson Buffett Foundation. She attended the University of Nebraska-Lincoln, and because she was a great scholar, Brenda earned $500 each semester until she graduated. Including Brenda, about 450 black students attending college benefitted from the Buffett Scholarship. Brenda went on to law school, returned to Omaha and captured a great job. Brenda also leaned into her natural interest of community empowerment. During that time, we became even better friends. Brenda is largely responsible for Pinkney Street becoming very popular in Omaha.

Brenda and her husband still reside on Pinkney Street. There was something special about this street. Famed Heisman Trophy winner and University of Nebraska-Lincoln football standout, Johnny Rogers, grew up on this street. Although several blocks away, my buddy Gibson's first home was also on Pinkney Street.

Our family house at 24th and Pinkney was positioned in the middle of the block and it seemed never too far from the places we often traveled.

Angeline's family's church, Clair United Methodist Church, was just around the corner from our home. There were great families on Pinkney Street. Many of the kids really stood out because of their personalities or academic and athletic achievements. I organized a bowling league for teenagers and coached softball teams.

While teaching Sunday school at Clair United Methodist Church, it was there that I met three young men who became the stars of our softball team. Related to me through marriage, Jerry and Ronnie Bartee, are the sons of Louise Bartee who was Angeline's second cousin. Howard Duncan, was the first cousin of the Bartees and son of a great man who we affectionately called "Dunc." Those guys along with Willis Warren, a Pinkney Street resident, endured a different degree of racial discrimination than I experienced. Yet, as innocent as a softball game among 12 and 13-year-old boys, yielded an ad in an Iowa newspaper. Our team was the only one identified by race instead of a team name.

Pinkney Street was the place where I held insightful conversations about the victories and injustices around Omaha. I appreciated other points of view and I recall especially being engaged in an ongoing dialogue with one neighbor about the pros and cons of violence versus non-violence positions our civil rights leaders espoused against our common enemies. Often, I would have strong arguments with one of my neighbors, Muhammed X, about our opposite points-of-view on politics and civil disobedience. It was during the 1960-61 period and I was adamant about implementing non-violent and peaceful protests.

It took a pivotal situation involving black Muslim men who were killed in a fight with Omaha police officers. The surviving Muslim men were sentenced to life in prison. Given the circumstances involved in the deaths of the Muslim men, I began to accept that not all peaceful protests are heard by the instigators of the severe violence. It was a shift in my perspective, yet I maintained a hard stance on non-violence.

I also vividly remember this time because my wife, Angeline, changed her hair style in 1962. She cut off her long, brown hair and traded it for an afro. It caused a stir in the community as she was the only other black woman – the first one being Bobbie Davis – to wear the afro style in Omaha. Soon, other black women were sporting their 'fros.

CHAPTER ELEVEN

We Shall Overcome

Zion Baptist Church in the 1950s.
(Photo courtesy of the Durham Museum)
Source: Omaha History

The early 1960s was a highly charged period as the civil rights movement made its way to Omaha. Revs. Rudolph McNair and Kelsey Jones founded the Citizens Civic Committee for Civil Liberties or 4CL. Every Sunday for about three years, we packed up the family after finishing our midday post-church dinner and headed for Zion Baptist Church at 22nd and Grant Street; not far from our home. The purpose of the 4CL was to inform and embody us with dynamic non-violent resistance techniques in the persistent battle against racism, repressions, and discrimination towards Negroes in Omaha.

We received news from across the nation about the oppressions directed toward black people. It was electric as there was a speaker who always warmed up the audience with his announcements. Often, we sang songs familiar with the civil rights movement. We learned the right way to lock our arms with one another. I loved it because our family was together. Candy, Gene and Nieve were sitting right there with Angeline and I. Missy was a baby and we left her with either a grandmother or with sister-in-law, Greta Owen.

The 4CL was about action. Our first major target was the Woolworth five-and-dime store. It prohibited Negroes from eating at its lunch counter. The lunch counter policy was that Negroes had to stand up and wait until the whites were finished sitting and eating. It was 1962 and the first sophisticated and peaceful march against discrimination in Omaha shut down that store. We marched in twos during those May and June months in downtown Omaha at Farnam and 16th streets. We numbered 300 and were mostly comprised of Negroes and a few whites. This lasted several weeks until Negroes could eat food at the counter alongside our white brethren. We also marched against another retailer committing injustices toward Negroes.

At Brandeis department stores, if Negroes tried on coats to see whether it fit them, they were obligated to buy the coats. The same thing was true of shoes and other apparel.

The year 1964 was a big year for me, but a bigger year for my buddy, Gibson. He was the star pitcher for the St. Louis Cardinals, and he won the World Series by beating the New York Yankees in seven games. Gibson set Omaha on fire. Who would think that a poor boy from the housing projects would achieve such an incredible status? Of course, he was always kind, and even visited Mason School where I taught. He was a big hero, and he was really appreciated. He was always modest around me and has always been a shy guy. He would seem to be aloof with people that he met as an adult and those that he knew as a youngster. He did not understand all the glamour and other attention that came with him. It was a perplexing problem for him and our black brothers and sisters in Omaha.

My association with Gibson worked out well for me as I was able to get more involved in more programs in the Omaha Public Schools system. Warren Franke came by my classroom at Mason and he interviewed me for Council Bluffs newspaper called the Daily Nonpareil. That is an interesting name for a newspaper as "nonpareil" means not equal. He did a big article on my volunteer work with the youth, particularly with many athletes like Johnny Rodgers, Ron Boone, and many others.

Me and Johnny Rodgers in the newspaper

Ron also grew up in the same housing development that I did (Logan Fontenelle), attended Tech High School, where like NBA's Bob Boozer and MLB's Bob Gibson, Ron was coached by the same man who saw great potential in him. Ron eventually became a professional basketball player where he never missed a game. Today, he is the Utah Jazz's on-air announcer.

Warren's article caused my picture to be in a newspaper for the first time. The picture included a young white student looking up at me which got over to the black community in Omaha and it made me quite popular.

Among the many interests I loved was to hang out at Goodwin's Spencer Street Barber Shop with my lifelong friend Daniel Goodwin and Ernie Chambers, who later became a Nebraska state senator. It looked like we were going to make some social and economic progress in our beloved Omaha community.

Another lifelong friend, respected journalist and community activist, Charles B. Washington and with help and that of others, Washington and others, Father Jim Stewart was a big wheel in the country. He selected me as his community organizer for the Omaha Archdiocese's Catholic Social Action Office. This was the biggest employment break that I had so far. I left the Nebraska Psychiatric Institute and Mason School behind and became an activist in the Omaha community. I made enough money to drop the part-time job at the YMCA and was beginning to enjoy a different life. We loved our new home, and the kids were being active at the local grade school. I was finally off onto a whole different dimension in life.

Father Stewart was a big wheel in the country. He knew every major activist inside and outside of the Catholic Church. He introduced me to one of the greatest community organizers in the country.

His name was Saul Alinsky, an Eastern European immigrant who invented community organizing in Chicago in the 1930s. His mentee, Thomas Gaudette, was a fierce Chicago community organizer who was known for his tough tactics against slumlords and drug-infested communities. They liked my style of community organization in Omaha. Alinsky's amazing work, defending the rights of immigrants in Chicago who worked in horrid conditions in the meatpacking industry at the city's stockyards, led to the founding of the Back of the Yards Neighborhood Council in 1939. The strong community action organization scored many victories against worker oppression and it also backed the school lunch programs for children. Even Alinsky's book, Rules for Radicals: A Pragmatic Primer for Realistic Radicals was what President Barack Obama carried with him when he was a community organizer on the south side of Chicago.

After I trained with Alinsky and Gaudette in Chicago, they joined us in Omaha in 1965. They were fully equipped to organize the community and worked hard for the Catholic Social Action Office. We were a formidable team with Father Stewart at the helm as a master teacher. We followed a strategic plan to place one half of Omaha's inner-city black community in a newly named area, Kellom Community Council. It was located on one side of 24th Street east to 26th Street. The other half of the community was renamed the Lake-Charles Organization and it was geographically bound by Cummings to Lake streets. Our goal was to rid our communities of poverty, despair, slumlords, and other evils that entrap poor folk.

We were really organizing my dear Omaha communities. In my role with the Catholic Social Action Office, we were fortunate to become one of the nation's first recipients of a grant to receive 20 community involvers through Volunteers for Service to America (VISTA.) The volunteers were intended to be in Omaha for two years to help us organize communities around a common mission. Ten of them were assigned to the Kellom Community Council and ten were placed with the Lake-Charles Organization. We found housing for them in formerly vacant housing in the black community. We had a rough start as we had to interpret to the black residents that the white people were volunteers interested in helping to improve our communities.

The VISTA volunteers were the energy and people power that we needed to make great progress. I was able to establish the first, all-day daycare. We also needed a building for the daycare center. We looked all throughout the community and we found a perfect locale, a vacant and rundown place that used to be a vibrant retail store where my mother used to trade. I made the decision that we would purchase the former Marsh retail location because it was ideally situated in the community. Since we did not have ready funds to buy the building, it became my first challenge to raise money for a worthy community cause. There were many naysayers who told me, "Wead, you're crazy. You cannot do it. You will never get the money for a "day" retail location ideally situated in the community. We purchased the daycare center." We did.

VISTA's Bernie Hyde and Nancy Spencer showed such passion and were heavily involved in the detail work to ensure that all Lake-Charles Organization's programs were enacted. They always rolled up their sleeves to help in all projects. The two became a couple and married in December 1967. Nancy said, "we met when we were serving as VISTA volunteers in Omaha, Nebraska ... under Rod Wead's leadership."

The Kellom Community Council included some hearty VISTAs, including Bob Tyson. Bob captured the community's progress through his exceptional photography while serving during the 1966 riots. Bob, Nancy, and Bernie were kind enough to journey from their homes in California and Virginia to join me during my Omaha street dedication in 2018. Bob reflected on how they assisted me in community organizing.

Sometimes my workday would extend to 15 hours. Still, I was able to maintain a healthy balance in my life. While I was very busy, my wife, Angeline, made sure that our kids were well taken care of.

No matter how busy I was, we always ate dinner as a family at 6 p.m. And it was always a nice meal. Between 1962 – 1972, when I traveled a lot, Angeline made sure our kids had normalcy. I remembered the advice of Dr. Yarr from the Nebraska Psychiatric Institute where Dr. Yarr and I worked. He said to always have dinner with my children. He said that I would really know my kids by breaking bread and talking with them about what was going on in their lives.

Our dinner table was a laboratory for the "programming" of our kids into their future lives. To the left, sat our oldest, Candy. Across from her and to my right was our son, Gene. Angeline sat at the other end of the table and on her right was our youngest, Missy. Across from Missy sat our middle child, Nieve. Listening and reading them very carefully, I pretty much knew what they were going to become in their adult lives. All four of them are very successful. Not necessarily because of me, but due to their mother being there and supporting them and me. She was the straw that stirred everything. I knew that they were receiving a good learning experience and it was due to their mother who was strict about the right things.

My stable home life afforded me the greatest gift; Working in the community that I grew up in was simply a privilege.

CHAPTER TWELVE

Modeling Rich Ideas in Poor Communities

VISTA Volunteer Bob Tyson, 1966, with community members

of the Lake-Charles Organization.

I was proud and humbled by the countless hours of planning and organizing to produce the very successful Lake Charles Daycare Center. It was well-run and quickly became a model for other daycare facilities in the Midwest. The other major project that was noteworthy was the "Pocket Playground." The first step was purchasing the lots for $1. Vista volunteer Nancy Spencer, named the play areas because of the small size of the lots -- usually the former site of a small home -- where we would place the equipment for the children. We organized the nation's first pocket playgrounds, which were converted from vacant, rat-infested lots into vibrant areas for kids in our economically poor neighborhoods.

We had several issues we had to deal with when organizing the pocket playgrounds. One of the biggest issues was that the lots were infested with rats. To correct this issue, we came up with a program borrowed from Alinsky's similar initiatives in Kansas City, Missouri; Chicago and Decatur, Illinois; and Akron, Ohio. The program was called "Ten Cents a Rat." We acquired gunny sacks to catch them. The funding came from the Catholic Church and we were able to pay the kids to catch and kill rats. Block by block, these kids were innovative in ridding the areas of rats. The mayor authorized the city's waste trucks to collect the rats and dispose of them. We increased the bounty to 25 cents per rat by receiving additional funding from the Catholic Archdiocese.

We wanted to put in swings, a teeter-totter and a slide at the first site at 28th & Grant streets. But we did not have the money to do it. Yet as the Lord would have it, someone introduced me to an outstanding man named Nick Newman. He was the youngest of three Newmans who owned five large grocery stores called Hinky Dinky. Nick and I became close almost "overnight." What a great man who happened to be Jewish. He paid for the playground equipment. You could see and feel the early signs of neighborhood empowerment. The neighbors volunteered to cut the grass and help with the loads of dirt to secure the best grounding for the playground. The VISTA volunteers installed all the playground equipment.

I remember it like it was yesterday when Nick came to see that first site. He was genuinely touched. We repeated that feat four more times. Nick paid for the equipment at all the sites. The pocket playgrounds made national news. A community organizer from Los Angeles, Dr. Walt Bremond, visited our playgrounds. He replicated it in his hometown. I will always remember that the same year the nation's schools were ordered to be integrated, we introduced the pocket playgrounds. That was 1964.

There was another issue and that was we needed a headquarters for our 20 volunteers and for other community activities. We found a rundown building, which was a former Jewish bathhouse. It was in poor shape, but we cleaned it up, painted it and made other repairs while leasing the building at 25th and Charles streets. As we were phasing in our move, strong anti-Semitic comments were brewing by some black neighbors. It was revealed that we were being charged an unreasonable monthly rent for the decrepit place.

My friend, Nick Newman again came to our rescue. He worked out an arrangement with the landlord as we were no longer charged the $45 for the monthly rent. In a small yet significant way, Nick helped along Black-Jewish relations by sticking his neck out to get a landlord to do the right thing. From that location, we were able to produce some of the finest papers in the country called the Lake-Charles Action. It was a bi-weekly paper and people could not wait for it to come off the press. It was popular because we produced excellent stories about the neighborhoods, and the slumlords and the city council persons – most of them were very racist -- and we would expose them.

We talked about the superhighway that was coming through the black community. It ripped our community apart. The paper fought it. We did not win the battle on this transportation issue.

The paper was known for rubbing raw the sores of discontent. We had a three-year run with this paper.

We accomplished so much in a short time. Yet, it was time for me to move on.

CHAPTER THIRTEEN

Making Moves

My dream job came true at Wesley House.
Source: United Methodist Community Centers

There was a citywide search for an executive director of one of the highest profile non-profit agencies that was committed to dramatically improving the communities in which it served. I believed that I was ideally suited as a candidate because I was an active United Methodist Church member through my home church, Clair UMC, was a product of the poorest neighborhoods and because of my pure passion to improve the lives of the collective community. I was also a proven community activist and accomplished tangible results by the time I interviewed for the job at the United Methodist Community Centers, based at Wesley House on Parker Street in North Omaha. Just as I was preparing for my interview, an unusual problem arose. Thank God it did not turn out to be disastrous.

Gibson was scheduled to pitch the key game for the St. Louis Cardinals in the 1968 World Series. Gibson asked me if I would please attend that game and I said that I would. Coincidentally, the interview committee at Wesley House scheduled my interview for the same day as the World Series game. I told them my dilemma and they thankfully rescheduled the interview. I was on cloud nine when the announcement was made that I was hired to lead Wesley House.

When I told Angeline, she and I cried real tears.

The location of Wesley House was ideal. It was just two blocks away from the house that we had built, and it allowed me to have breakfast, walk to work and be near my kids' elementary school, Franklin Elementary.

Wesley House was the oldest United Methodist community agency in the country. It was formerly called the Omaha City Missions. We acquired another similar community center in South Omaha, so we called ourselves the United Methodist Community Centers. We worked hard to keep the Woodson Center alive. It was once directed by a very popular director, Alice Wilson.

I became busy immediately. There were many new requirements of me and expectations for the growth of Wesley House. I remember having to change board members and recruit new ones. My first hire was June Swanigan. She was a crackerjack secretary and became an administrative assistant. She was very bright. I knew her from my grade school years. She had children and still worked long hours.

She was so good at letters and organization, which were key to the launch and sustainment of programs that became nationally known.

It seemed that all the stars were lined up for this poor boy from the housing projects. The most exciting years of my entire professional life was during my time with the Wesley House. We were really grooving and excited about those economic ventures.

We had outdoor movies on our campus. Kids from all over the community would come and see first-rate movies and watch them from their blankets. We had the first Juneteenth parade and the "Stone Soul Picnic" sponsored by the Wesley House group. It was the guest speakers' program that was a community favorite and was organized by Charlie Washington, editor-in-chief of the Omaha Star, a weekly newspaper for the black community. The Omaha Star was the only black newspaper in Nebraska that was founded by newspaper owner and publisher, the great Mildred Brown.

It seemed like Charlie knew everybody throughout the country. He brought in speakers such as author, historian and founder of Chicago's DuSable Museum, Margaret Burroughs. Activists Stokely Carmichael (Kwame Ture), Fannie Lou Hamer, "Little Rock Nine's" Ernest Green, Ralph Bunche, James Brown, and many others to our beloved agency. They educated and entertained the black community.

These events proved to be fine cultural events for our community. Nick Newman, owner of a local grocery store chain, and who I had befriended from my days with the Lake-Charles Organization, was more than happy to assist me in fundraising for our projects.

The angel from the Dundee area, Susan "Susie" Thompson Buffett, also emerged to get involved and greatly assist with our Wesley House initiatives. Susie and I attended the same high school, Omaha Central High School, and we knew of each other casually.

But we became quite close during my early months of employment at Wesley House.

Susie also afforded me the opportunity to continue my personal development in researching black history.

The first trip that she sponsored for me was to the New York Public Library Schomburg Center for Research in Black Culture. I subsequently went to several of the great libraries and visited many museums. During that time, there were many sit-ins and other protests going on around the country and I was able to gain great intellectual perspective while participating in many grassroots activities.

With Susie and Warren's support, we had many outstanding programs with origins at Wesley House.

I became closely affiliated with the Black Community Developers, an outreach program led by a wonderful man, Dr. Rev. Negail Riley. Negail was motivated by the great Kwame Toure (Stokely Carmichael). Kwame Toure inspired us to do many interesting things on behalf of the black cause and I became deeply involved in that while serving as the executive director of Wesley House.

Together with Negail and Kwame, I traveled to Vancouver, British Columbia (Canada) in 1976 to lobby the United Nations (U.N.) for fair, accessible and quality housing for economically poor citizens. It was quite a time as thousands of activists descended upon the Canadian community during the 12-day U.N. conference. Our voices were heard during sessions on "Habitat: The United Nations Conference on Human Settlement." Even though thousands of activists were there,

Negail, Kwame and I somehow attracted the most attention from U.S. law enforcement officials who followed us everywhere around the city.

The major, historic resolution became the forerunner to Habitat for Humanity International and National programs. The U.N. conference accepted 64 resolutions from global activists, including ours. It was quite a moment-in-time to stand before the August body and deliver ideas that were accepted and utilized. Given my developmental years of living in the Logan Fontenelle Housing Project community, I knew the importance of children having a decent place to live. Coincidentally, Habitat for Humanity of Omaha's main office is located exactly on the former site of my Logan Fontanelle homestead on north 24th Street. I took a walk around the Habitat property and could pinpoint where my good friends and I lived and played some 60 years earlier.

CHAPTER FOURTEEN

The Warren and Susie Buffett Effect in North Omaha

Warren and Susie Buffett as a young couple.

(Fold3 by Ancestry)

Source: Warren Buffett

The reality from the famous Charles Dickens' opening in the classic book, A Tale of Two Cities – "it was the best of times. It was the worst of times..." during my days as the head of the United Methodist Community Centers. The 1967 Omaha riots, that included lootings, fires, and other uprisings, mirrored those around the nation. That amount of destruction across the country and in Omaha was considered the worst since the Civil War period. Of course, I was involved in many situations as a non-violent leader. That year also marked the beginning of top financial investor Warren Buffett's behind-the-scenes involvement in similar causes of non-violent change for African Americans, Jewish Americans, and other disenfranchised people. Also, his wife, Susie, and her good friend, Rackie Newman, went straight to the powerful heads of the Omaha YMCA organization to make heavier investments in the poor neighborhoods. Rackie was the wife of Nick Newman, the owner of Hinky Dinky local grocery store chain.

Warren and Susie were invited to Grinnell College in Iowa for a convocation that included speakers Ralph Ellison, award-winning author (Invisible Man) and Nobel Peace Prize winner, Dr. Martin Luther King, Jr. Susie said that Dr. King's powerful words and perspective largely changed Warren. Later, Warren and Nick waged a deliberate, successful campaign to change the membership of the Omaha Club and Highland Country Club from exclusive to inclusive.

All the while, the United Methodist Community Center benefited when "Susie and Rackie sent black kids to summer camps and set up an interracial dialogue group for high school students. Wead had become a frequent presence in the Buffett household," Warren Buffett and Alice Schroeder, The Snowball: Warren Buffett and the Business of Life.

Warren and I talked more, and he fully supported Susie in her sincere work to improve the lives of folk in North Omaha. I believed that Warren and I were seeing eye-to-eye as he and I strategized on several causes. Just a few years ago, Warren referred to me eight times in his book, "Snowballed."

Susie had a hard-to-describe positive effect on the agency. I'd known Susie since our classmate days at Central High and she was always a giving person. That carried over to her involvement with Wesley House and the many programs supported by the Buffetts. It helped that she married a gentleman who owned a newspaper in the Benson area and had the gift of raising and making money. I honestly believed that with the involvement and investments of the Buffetts, the Newmans, and other 'good white and Jewish folk,' that it would be the spark to break the cycle of poverty in Omaha. I was obviously wrong as impoverished communities currently exist in even more dire situations than in my younger years. Yet, it did not keep me from trying to initiate other solutions to help propel black people in more profitable situations.

Warren established a lasting friendship with Gibson and those two men were among those I consulted with about the establishment of the nation's first black-owned AM & FM radio station. The emphasis is on AM & FM as that feat was highly unusual. With two grants totaling $11,000 and a loan of $250,000 provided by the United Methodist Church, we began to sell shares of stock in the radio station in early 1970. In March 1970, the investors from Omaha's black community purchased the radio stations, pending approval by the Federal Communications Commission.

The internal building of the staff included Cathy Liggins Hughes, who recruited and trained the initial DJs. Cathy, also a Buffett college scholarship recipient, once lived in the Logan Fontenelle Housing Projects near my home. I always considered her my little sister. Cathy was enthusiastic about the start of KOWH AM/FM and I thought she was going to be affiliated with the station for a long time. However, she was offered a position at Howard University at its WHUR-FM and TV station in Washington, D.C. She would work with the great Tony Brown before launching Radio One and later, TV One networks. Both are publicly owned and enormously successful.

It was a glorious day when we finally opened the station with a Diana Ross song featured as our inaugural music. It was operated for 24 hours a day. The black community was absolutely in love with its black-owned radio station.

There were more ventures in my vision. With the support of the United Methodist Church, I was focused on black capitalism as the next fulfillment of Dr. King's dream.

CHAPTER FIFTEEN

Winning Ways

Best friends since we were 10 years old: Gibson and me.

Source: The Wead Collection

I have been incredibly blessed to know and experience several great athletes in different sports, many of them becoming Hall of Famers. I grew up with or mentored some of the greatest athletes – Marion Hudson, Bob Gibson, Johnny Rodgers, Marlin Briscoe, Gayle and Roger Sayers, Bob Boozer and countless women who were not recognized in athlete feats because of their gender.

I was a decent athlete, lettering in three sports at Omaha Central High School, and accomplishing similar feats during my years at Dana College, where I was recognized in 1974 as one of its outstanding alumni based on my community development and college athletic accomplishments. I always remained close to athletics and recreational activities. During the great coaching years of the University of Nebraska-Lincoln's Bob Devaney, I became a season ticket holder. With my two tickets, I rotated each of my four children to attend the Saturday games with me. I believe it gave them a special appreciation for college sports.

Gibson and I played lots of sports and were on the winning Monarch Y softball team. In this 1951 picture, Gibson kneeled, third from left, on front row. I'm easy to spot on the back row.

Source: The Wead Collection

There were many standouts during the Devaney years, yet one player dominated the offensive stats: Number 20, Halfback Johnny Rodgers. Johnny's sophomore through senior years were marked with three Orange Bowl wins. He ran back a 77-yard punt in the 1972 Orange Bowl, the year Big Red became the undisputed national champions in both polls. In his senior year, Johnny ended his time at Nebraska with four touchdowns and one pass in the 1973 Orange Bowl.

I had known Johnny for several years. The Omaha native really impressed me with athleticism. I was introduced to him by our good friend, the late Charles B. Washington. Johnny has been like a little brother to me. He has accomplished so much off the University of Nebraska-Lincoln football field that he has yielded as much recognition as his former playing days.

One of the best attended events during my years at the United Methodist Community Centers was the Superstar banquets. Gibson was our inaugural banquet honoree in 1967. We also honored Gayle Sayers, Bob Boozer and Johnny Rodgers. Their accomplishments kept Omaha on the map, and they served as great role models to the youth who were coming of age during turbulent days of riots and police brutality.

CHAPTER SIXTEEN

....

Pushing for Progress

Mrs. Charlene Gibson, Attorney Wilbur Phillips and I sign
incorporation papers for KOWH-AM/FM

Source: Lincoln Journal

My very able and highly competent friend, Fannie "Mrs. G" Goodwin, was the president of the Lake-Charles Organization and was the guiding force behind the development of the pocket playgrounds. Fannie was also close to Susie Buffett. I had these two gems at my disposal along with the great Nick Newman and even greater, Charles "Charlie" B. Washington. Charlie gave me oodles of his time and advice.

We changed the structure of the United Methodist Community Center's largest agency, Wesley House. We created a black history library, and it housed several books and articles about black people. It was also a neat area for children to play in and we held programs in there. I also removed the basketball nets from the gym and turned it into an all-purpose room that housed many activities instead of only basketball. It became the Skinner Learning Center and was named after Mr. Eugene Skinner, who was known as OUR "Black Superintendent."

Rev. Harold Croom built a church across the parking lot from our center. Unfortunately, although Rev. Croom dreamed of an integrated community, the whites were moving out of the nice neighborhood that surrounded Wesley House. We took that church, we converted it and held so many activities in that building. We named that building the Bishop Noah W. Moore Building. He was the first black Methodist Bishop in Nebraska. He was a dear friend and fervent supporter of my work. Nick Newman and Warren Buffett were the funders of that building.

I was especially grateful for my promotion to lead the United Methodist Community Centers, with my main office being at Wesley House in North Omaha. My salary provided the needed money for Angeline to finish her bachelor's degree and do a little more for my kids. She was very active in changing the public-school system that never abided by the 1964 decision to equalize the education for black and white children. She was very active in education.

My job at Wesley House was the most important and best job in my life. It set me on the course of my career, and I became a popular figure in the country.

Susie's primary goal was to get kids in college and see them graduate. Her quest became so big that we hired a full-time to interview the inner-city youth and help them by tutoring them to get them prepared for college. That was a big success for our community, Wesley House and for the entire state of Nebraska.

The first scholarship recipient was Steve Sims. We graduated from Central High and went to the Storm King Prep School. He went onto to spend four years at Columbia University where he received both bachelor's and master's degrees. He enjoyed huge success in his career. Steve became our model for other young people in Omaha's inner city to emulate. They did.

Steve inspired hundreds of young people to apply and receive scholarships from the Susie Buffett Scholarship Fund. Susie and Warren did an incredible job of being role models and helping kids get college. Probably half of the youth would not have gotten to go to college had it not been for the Buffett funds. Oftentimes, Warren would mail bonds for us to cash in for our Wesley House programs and scholarship fund.

One of my ventures outside the walls of Wesley House, yet related to my mission, was to develop Franklin Community Federal Credit Union. It was primarily for low-income persons with the average loan cap of $300. It quickly grew into a multi-million institution.

Yet, I always longed to develop a radio station. It would be a radio station that was completely owned and operated by African Americans. Ever since I was a paperboy for the Omaha World- Herald, I always dreamed that someday I would develop a radio station that would "sock soul."

When Gibson were youngsters sitting along the curb and identifying cars that passed by, we would always identify the great Charlie Davis' car. It was a nice slick, 1948 Dodge. He would always stop and just say hi to us. Mr. Davis formed the Carver Savings &

Loan Company, and it went well. Because of the lack of full support, it was not as successful as it could be.

I was thinking that a community bank in Omaha would really galvanize all the resources we needed for a strong, north Omaha community. Susie Buffett, Charlene Gibson, my good friend and wife of my lifelong buddy Gibson, and a few others began to visualize a black-owned bank in North Omaha. I shared the vision with Warren Buffett. To my surprise, he was fully supportive of the black community raising its own capital and therefore, creating financial empowerment.

I got excellent advice from Warren on how to capitalize it and raise money. Warren knew a lot about banks, and he held several meetings with Gibson and me to see if we could get it going. Warren also convinced me to seek a state charter for the bank instead of a federal charter since the hurdles would be a lot less, thus less risk and the financial gains would be the same for the investors.

Warren refused to invest in what became the Community Bank of Nebraska, believing that black people should be the exclusive investors. Yet, once established, Warren sent considerable business to the bank and that propelled and sustained the profitability throughout the bank's existence.

After a long and tough money battle and going through all the necessary processes to establish a bank, we got one started. In June 1971, the articles of incorporation to establish the bank were filed with the Nebraska State Department of Bank and the Secretary of State. The Community Bank of Nebraska's charter was finalized on April 16, 1973 and opened for business 11 days later.

The Community Bank of Nebraska became the 36th black-owned bank in the United States. Omaha was one of a few cities that boasted a black-owned radio station and a black bank.

The Community Bank was several years in the making. When I embarked on the quest to raise a $500,000 in seed money for the bank. We brought $125,000 to the meeting to secure the Nebraska bank charter meeting. The commissioner charged us to raise the balance of the seed money before opening. In a relatively short time, we raised another $375,000 and received the state bank charter.

Herbert Patton, a good friend and trusted colleague of mine, is credited for naming the bank. He felt the best name for the bank would be the Community Bank of Nebraska.

The bank was organized and emanated out of a trailer at 60th and Ames Avenue. I never dreamed that several years later in 2018, a street would be named for me near the original site of the Community Bank of Nebraska.

People were elated that the small community, Omaha – with about 40,000 black folk - would have a black-owned radio station, a black-owned bank, and a black-owned credit union.

It was quite a time for all of Omaha, especially black Omaha. We attracted national media and shored up partnerships with many community-based organizations. One networks. One important recognition of how significant the lineup of economic progress was for the black community came in the fall of 1973. That is when 70 black church leaders from around the country, met in Omaha as part of a multi-city program to discuss and examine best practices of community development. My good friend, the Rev. Dr. Negail Riley, Assistant General Secretary for Minority Concerns, National

Division, United Methodist Board of Global Ministries, heaped praise upon my efforts with the support of Methodism.

"Without a doubt, Rodney Wead is one of the outstanding black church men in the country," Negail said at the time of the conference.

I was honored that 70 participants in the conference listened intently and toured with a context the community credit union, radio station and community bank in Omaha. It was a gratifying feeling, especially because I had undergone a vicious and untrue period of accusations that I somehow had something to do with "missing money" from KOWH AM-FM radio station. The lie sunk my spirits. I was fortunate that honorable members of the Omaha community stood up for me. Charlene Gibson, for one, disliked public attention and she did a great job staying away from the limelight. Yet she held a press conference and denounced the lies against me, and others joined in. I cannot tell you how grateful I felt, yet I still felt discouraged.

That is where my good friend, Charles Washington stepped in. His invitation to the one-and-only Duke Ellington to visit Omaha was accepted. Boy, did seeing the Duke cheer me up! After he played a few sets for a private audience at Allen's Showcase, the Duke and I walked together along Lake Street to the Mildred Brown Coronation Dance Hall and onward to my car. It was during this stroll that the Duke shared how the "A Train" became one of the most beloved and popular tunes associated with the great maestro. What a privilege that was for me. I got to walk with the "Duke" all by myself. It was just the inspiration that I needed to carry on my work. Indeed, I did.

CHAPTER SEVENTEEN

Chicago: My Kind of Town

Image by Jürgen Polle Pixabay

I was beginning to think there were perhaps other mountains to climb. Little did I know that although Lerone Bennett and I became friends while I was in Omaha, that he and I would become partners in a big project in Chicago. The Community Renewal Society did an expansive search for a new executive. They asked me to come to Chicago for an interview. The Rev. Bob Alward, a minister of the United Church of Christ in Omaha, moved to Chicago and became a member of the board of the Community Renewal Society, a United Church of Christ foundation. He recommended me for the position as did Susie Buffett.

As the Most High would have it, I was chosen as the associate director of the Community Economic Development Division. After much consultation with family and lots of prayers, I decided to embark on a new career with new mountains to climb in Chicago. I joined that fine agency in 1972. It was then a 100-year-old agency and endowed by a bank in Chicago. It had a $20 million foundation. Chicago is a city of broad shoulders and incredibly bright and talented African Americans. I was fortunate to have some of that money to give away to fledgling organizations and churches. I immediately became involved in many dynamic programs in Chicago. I achieved a lot while in Chicago.

Over an eight-year period, I organized 80 food co-ops in the housing projects of Chicago. We were based in the Cabrini-Green Homes. I was very fortunate to have a dynamic staff of people who believed in my philosophy of cooperative economics and we organized food cooperatives for low-income folk. We purchased food at the wholesale price at a large cooperative and in turn, sold the food at a low cost. It saved participants as much as 30 – 40 percent on their food bills. This remains one of my favorite programs.

Another major initiative was for me to become president of the Center for Neighborhood Technology. Scott Bernstein was the single staff member, and we had a great time educating the community on different types of technology. We produced a handbook that was called, the Neighborhood Economy. We suggested opportunities and strategies that could create jobs for local community residents. In that same vein, we developed the idea of planting tomatoes on some of the flat rooftops in Chicago. We used the hydroponic method. It was very successful, and we planted and grew many tomatoes on the rooftops of the Uptown community.

I was extremely blessed to meet a dynamic minister, the Rev. Jeremiah Wright, and our agency was able to allocate a $100,000 loan to his fine church, Trinity United Church of Christ. He continued as a successful minister. The great former United States President Barack Obama was a member of Trinity.

Another extraordinary program that I helped to found was the nation's third Black United Fund (BUF). BUF is a philanthropic organization that distributes monies to communities around Chicago that otherwise are ignored or not funded at all by larger charities. I was able to work with friend and fraternity brother Lerone Bennett, longtime Chicago Congressman Danny K. Davis, and Ken Vaughn, who worked for another large Chicago foundation. Lerone was able to get the famous publisher John H. Johnson to contribute the first $10,000 to the Black United Fund. That was great leverage for us to raise more money for our community. Hugh Hefner was also active in helping us raise funds using his fabulous Playboy Mansion. We held fundraisers there. He made many contributions to the black community, and especially to Black United Fund.

> *Lerone and I were also able to help put together the first $200,000 program to renovate the famous DuSable Museum of Margaret Burroughs who is best known for her famous poem, "What Shall I Tell My Children Who are Black?"*

Next, we developed a low-wattage FM station in the South Shore community. It reached about four or five square miles in that South Side Chicago community. The annual budget was around $1 million. It was not financially sustainable, and we closed it.

A wonderful project that promised sustained economic development was the New Horizon Plastic Corp., a manufacturing plant located in the heart of a rough community at 40th and Wabash Ave. It was a 50,000-square-foot facility that molded plastic cups for healthcare organizations. It operated 7-day per week, 24-hour shifts. Within five years, New Horizon received a sizable contract from Kraft Foods for production of 4.5 million plastic margarine lids. That massive order allowed the plant to expand to utilize five presses.

Unexpected economic factors put financial pressure on New Horizons. The 1974-75 oil embargo, raw materials shortages, large utility bills and overcapitalization, caused the once thriving operation to fall behind in its payments to private creditors and to the U.S. Small Business Administration. In the fall of 1975, after six years of operations, New Horizons closed.

Beyond the CRS funding that spurred sustainable projects, I was fortunate to work closely with top community organizers and activists Bobby Rush, now a U.S. Congressman and former member of the Black Panther Party. He along with the late Rev. Leon Finney Jr., spearheaded the efforts to elect the city of Chicago's first black mayor, Harold Washington. It was one of my fondest accomplishments in Chicago.

CHAPTER EIGHTEEN

Moving Back to Go Forward

I had an incredible 10 years in Chicago. I acquired my master's degree in community development at Roosevelt University, and my doctorate in cooperative economics from the Union Graduate School. Its curriculum was attached to Roosevelt.

While there were many accomplishments, I had a few downers. My now former wife, Angeline, and I parted company. That was a sad experience certainly for both of us. Our separation occurred after we both returned to Omaha in order for me to return to my old job at Wesley House. While in Chicago, I received a call that I was wanted and needed to get back to Omaha to move things along. It was also a perfect time to be there for my mother whose health was failing.

Back to Angeline and me: I tried to the best of my ability to reconcile with her and convince her to come back with me to Omaha and try to start over again. That was a mistake on my part for suggesting it. She left her fine job at South Shore Community Bank in Chicago. After Angeline and I separated, she left for Atlanta to live with my middle daughter, Nieve, and her family. As far as I know, Angeline is doing very fine now.

I was in Omaha for a while at Wesley House and as a single man. As I was adjusting to my "new" life, I got to be quite busy with a program; Sweat Equity Housing which was something I developed in Chicago. I thought I could bring that program to Omaha. The program was designed for women who would get their housing for free, and they could work in their homes to pay for their homes – through sweat equity. My friend, Omaha Mayor Mike Boyle was very interested in this program that was directly headed by Mike Maroney.

While in Omaha during this time, I taught at Creighton University and at the University of Nebraska Omaha. It was also during this time that my dear mother, who I loved so much, passed on. My great friend Charles Washington passed on too. After that, I experienced some lonely and sad times.

Some good people in Columbus, Ohio sought me out and I agreed to an interview with The Neighborhood House there.

At the same time, I met my present wife, Vanessa Tutt, on October 26, 1990. I considered that a good sign because that was my mother's birthdate.

I gave her a small birthday party at Crown Point Tower Rehab Center in Omaha, in which she also lived. After the party, I visited my Mom and sat in my favorite seat next to her bed. My Mom suggested that I should treat myself to some music. She suggested that I have a good time at one of my favorite places, The Allen Showcase, a famous jazz nightclub, located on the near northside of Omaha. Mom always presented good, viable options for me all of my life. This suggestion proved to be a good one.

I must make a quick digression to highlight the Allen Showcase. The famous Allen Showcase was founded about 1948 by a successful and wonderful entrepreneur, Paul Allen. Omaha is located ideally in the Midwest of the U.S. so the best African American entertainers would perform there. Allen Showcase had headliners who included Count Basie, Duke Ellington, Pearl Bailey, Sammy Davis, Jr., Nat King Cole, and scores of great black talents. I was always a loyal customer of Allen Showcase, beginning in my late teen years. The great Paul Allen allowed me to patronize his place before I was 21 years old, which was the official legal age then to visit nightclubs.

On this evening in 1990, I walked into the famous Showcase and viewed a very nice-looking lady seated with a row of drinks in front of her. I inquired around the Showcase's ballroom about her and found out that her last name used to be Hardeman. I stood behind her waiting for a seat next to her to become available. When I seized the opportunity to sit next to her, I said "Good evening, Ms. Hardeman, my name is Rodney Wead." She replied something like, "You may have been one of my teachers at Tech High School." I was crushed! Yet, not to be defeated, I asked her about her background. She was a native Omahan and she was at the Showcase with her daughter, Tasha, who was celebrating her birthday, which was October 26th. It was also my mother's birthday. I gave her my telephone numbers and waited two weeks for her to call me. She called me in the middle of November.

We became engaged a few months later. A year later, we married at my good friend, Gibson's home on December 7, 1991. In between all this great excitement in my life, I was offered a great opportunity in Columbus, Ohio. After a short honeymoon, we then journeyed to Columbus, Ohio by driving there from Omaha.

My new position was executive director of a settlement house known as The Neighborhood House. I really enjoyed the work through the Neighborhood House. I founded Juneteenth in that city. It became so big that it outgrew our campus at The Neighborhood House. Juneteenth continues to this day. I was also able to work with several people who worked in the reform system. I was able to get four of the inmates at the city and county jails to paint portraits of famous women in Columbus and around the country. They were huge, 7" x 10" portraits. We found a building and we called it the Toni Morrison Place and that is where the 25 portraits of black women were hung. It was an exciting project.

Meanwhile, I wrote my third book; Coming This Far by Faith (January 1, 1996) and I dedicated it to my fraternity, Kappa Alpha Psi Fraternity, Inc.

It was about the history of the 25 African American churches in Columbus. It remains active reading for many Columbus residents. The black church has provided the pattern for the organization of mutual aid societies and insurance companies. As an editorial note, I urged the Columbus black church denominations to interact and make a dynamic presence to "break with past practices that the various denominations refused to make."

I chose the name of the book based on the great "Negro" spiritual that I heard often while growing up Pentecostal in Omaha. The words of the song were penned in the mid-1950s by little known, yet powerful Gospel musician, Albert A. Goodson. His words in the song resonated with me. It was also a processional song of my married family's Clair United Methodist Church's gospel choir, which was led by the late great Howard Duncan and his sisters Rosanna Duncan and Louise Bartee. The first stanza continues to move me.

WE'VE COME THIS FAR BY FAITH
First Line:
We've come this far by faith, leaning on the Lord
Song Key: F
Language: English
Authors: Albert A. Goodson

I just checked on the availability of Coming This Far by Faith outside of libraries and churches. It is considered "out of print-limited availability." My book is also featured in the authors collection of high school alma mater, Omaha Central High School.

CHAPTER NINETEEN

By God's "Grace"

0050C.01 House Resolution No. 33 Whereas, the members of the Missouri House of Representatives pause to recognize Rodney S. Wead, Ph.D., of St. Louis, Missouri, upon his retirement from Grace Hill Settlement House after a successful career that has spanned more than forty years; and Whereas, in his role as President and Chief Executive Officer since 1997, Dr. Wead has been responsible for the supervision of eleven neighborhoods in the City of St. Louis, St. Louis County, and St. Charles County, a budget of approximately $16 million, and programs that focus on neighborhood organization, family and child support, health, housing and economic development; and Whereas, an African-American and religious historian with expertise in urban studies, Dr. Wead holds a Bachelor of Science degree in History and Education from Dana College in Blair, Nebraska; a Master of Arts degree in Urban Studies from Roosevelt University in Chicago, Illinois; and a Doctorate in Sociology from The Union Institute in Cincinnati, Ohio; and Whereas, prior to his affiliation with Grace Hill Settlement House, Dr. Wead served as the Executive Director of Neighborhood House, Inc., in Columbus, Ohio, from 1992 to 1997; interim Professor of Black Studies at the University of Omaha, Nebraska, from 1991 to 1992; Executive Director of the

United Methodist Community Center, Inc., in Omaha from 1983 to 1991; Associate Professor of Sociology at Creighton University in Omaha from 1987 to 1992; Associate Executive Director of Community Renewal Society of Chicago from 1974 to 1983; and Executive Director of the United Methodist Centers, Inc., in Omaha from 1968 to 1974; and Whereas, an active member of countless organizations including Kappa Alpha Psi Fraternity, the National Head Start Association, and the Techni-Color Coalition, Dr. Wead is the proud recipient of numerous awards and honors, including the 2001 United Neighborhood Centers Award of Merit, 2001 Old North Neighborhood Special Distinguished Award, 2002 Kappa Alpha Psi Outstanding Achievement Award, 1993 Columbus Public Schools Golden Rule Award, and the 1991 Malcolm X Award, just to name a few; and Whereas, Dr. Wead is exceedingly proud of the many publications he has authored that include "M.O.R.E. - A Viable Self-Help Option for Low Income Communities, presented in Rotterdam, Netherlands, in 2002; "Giving a Gift That Multiplies", the St. Louis Post Dispatch, 1998; "Tribute to Martin Luther King", the St. Louis Post Dispatch, 1997; "Juneteenth", the St. Louis American, 1996; "Tribute to Martin Luther King", St. Louis American, 2000; and "Frederick Douglass", the Omaha World Herald, 1985: Now, there-fore, be it resolved that we, the members of the Missouri House of Representatives, Ninety-second General Assembly, unanimously join in expressing our utmost appreciation to Dr. Wead for his four de-cades of unparalleled service to settlement houses throughout the na-tion and in wishing him the long, rewarding, and enjoyable retirement he so richly deserves; and Be it further resolved that the Chief Clerk of the Missouri House of Representatives be instructed to prepare a properly inscribed copy of this resolution for Dr. Rodney S. Wead, as a mark of our esteem for him. Offered by Representative Juanita Head Walton District No. 81 I, Catherine L. Hanaway, Speaker of the House of Representatives, Ninety-second General Assembly, First Regular Session, do certify that the above is a true and correct copy of House Resolution No. 33, adopted January 10, 2003.

Catherine L. Hanaway, Speaker

Vanessa and I were planning for my retirement in Columbus, Ohio when the largest center in the U.S., the Grace Hill Settlement House, conducted a national search for an executive director. Vanessa and I were quite satisfied in Columbus. We just purchased a beautiful home, and we were settling down. But the people at Grace Hill were persistent. They made me an offer that I could not refuse, and they selected me to become the president and CEO of the Grace Hill Settlement House and Health Centers.

Grace Hill was a $32 million organization with many small health centers spread on the east side of St. Louis. I immediately formed the Women's Business Center of Grace Hill. It was part of the SBA's Women's Division. We worked with women who were interested in becoming entrepreneurs. It was very successful and each year, we won an award for the women who were successful with their businesses. We also received some seed monies.

I also went on to organize cottage industries for women. I got the idea from a successful businesswoman with national acclaim. It worked out quite well in St. Louis. I was also interested in the Head Start program. We wrote and received a $6 million grant and we partnered with the Urban League and we established some fine Head

Start programs throughout St. Louis. I was active of the Anniversary Club and later became president for two year, the oldest club in St. Louis. It began in 1865 and chartered in 1895. I was proud to be the first non-St. Louisan to be the president of this organization. I am still a member.

I left Grace Hill in 2000 and joined the faculty at Forest Park Community College. I am still an adjunct at that fine community college. I have taught more than 18 years in black history and sociology and had the opportunity to inspire and educate young black youth in this great city. St. Louis as a community, does not emphasize black history. It is a pleasure to get the students from Forest Park and others to share in black history.

African and American Black History are my passions. I am fortunate that my church, Cote Brilliante Presbyterian Church in St. Louis, provided me a platform to host lectures and movie nights of black-themed work to share the rich and powerful history of our people.

I am writing this amidst the 2020 Coronavirus pandemic and all the campus and church doors are shut down. Yet, I was involved in a wonderful, hour long Zoom meeting with young people around the nation, where I was able to share some slices of my life and answer great questions from them. It gave me confidence in our future.

I have a cousin who I met when I arrived in St. Louis in 1998. Her name is Madeline Wilks Matthews. She just turned 90-years-old. I became involved in her church, Cote Brilliante Presbyterian Church. I am delighted that I joined the church and remain active with this outstanding pastor, Rev. Clyde Crumpton. I have conducted several black history seminars at the church and have enjoyed the opportunity.

*The Dr. Rodney S. Wead street naming remains one of the
highlights of my life, September 2018
Source: The Wead Collection, Omaha World-Herald*

The "fight" for racial justice, equality and truth is never ending. The following piece that was published by my high school alma mater, Omaha Central High School, in July 2020, garnered a lot of comments. It summarizes where I've been and what has greatly impacted me:

AFTERWORD

Dr. Wead: Look Backward at History to Move Forward in Progress

The Central High School Foundation

Written by Dr. Rodney S. Wead

Class of 1953; Central High School Hall of Fame Inductee

June 24, 1969 was a hot summer day in Omaha, Nebraska; much like it is today. A group of Black youth were dancing to music in a vacant apartment at the Logan Fontenelle Housing Project in North Omaha. Carol Strong, a resident, spied the police nearby and heard that they were looking for a suspect who allegedly committed a robbery. She ran to the vacant apartment to alert the kids — especially her sister, Vivian Strong — that the cops were nearby. They immediately ran out of the apartment and toward their homes, not wanting to be caught up in confusion involving the police. Unfortunately, that's exactly what happened. Carol recalled hearing what sounded like firecrackers, and a flurry of young people running. When the chaos subsided, she saw her sister Vivian: lying on the ground, surrounded by her friends, a gunshot wound to the head at the hands of a white police officer.

I grew up in the Logan Fontenelle Housing Project, and often found myself in that same social space dancing with my friends. 20

years after my childhood was over, I listened to the tragic story of Vivian with my best friend, Bob Gibson, and I felt the story swing and hit close to home. My heart hurt deeply for the pain her family experienced. From all accounts, I heard that Vivian was a carefree young woman; certainly, undeserving of the violence with which she was murdered. Her senseless death shook our tight-knit Black Omaha community, leading to three days of riots calling for the abolition of police brutality. The community — our community — cried real tears for Vivian, and the people's anger intensified when we learned of the unequal justice that allowed the offending police officer to be released from jail on a mere $500 bond amid still-burning embers from the riots caused by Vivian's death. Several months later, the police officer's trial resulted in his full exoneration of manslaughter; he could rejoin the Omaha Police Department and remained employed until his retirement.

This remarkable moment in Omaha history illustrates the continuing conflict our local communities of color experience when confronted with law enforcement. What is more troubling is that our local experience is not unique; communities of color all across America express the same feelings of injustice and abuse. What's more, the recent surge of Black Lives Matter protests harken back to days of similar struggle: the Civil Rights Movement of the 1960's, which was a time of great anguish and great hope for the Omaha community, as well as for many Black communities across America. In fact, one year before Vivian was murdered, on May 4, 1968, I was severely beaten at a peaceful protest by plain-clothed Omaha police officers acting as private security officers of the then-American-Party Presidential Candidate and Alabama Governor, George Wallace.

What we learn from our examination of local and national history, from reflection on the personal experiences of others within our community, and from careful observation of the current movement for civil justice is this: the struggle against racism, police brutality, and other forms of injustice is not novel. It has been a sustained, hard-fought battle rooted in a deeply held commitment to the idea that 'all men are created equal.' The arch of our moral universe has been long, messy, and challenging — to loosely quote Dr. King — but it certainly bends in the direction of justice.

There is hope for our communities, now more than ever. Because people of all races have shown that they are willing to come together for the good of their neighbors.

As a civil rights activist now in my 80s, it is with battered breath and whispering humbleness I am requesting that all Centralites come together to stamp out racism and violence. And I have a few suggestions for how we can do that:

To disrupt the dominance of the white cultural perspective in our country, I believe that Black History should be mandatory for all K-12 students. Currently at Central High School, for example, African American History is offered as an elective course. For more than 25 years this course has educated diverse generations of Eagles on the struggles, successes, and achievements of black people throughout America's history. And it is only through this backwards examination of the diverse history of our nation that we can prepare ourselves to live life forward, meeting the challenges we are presented with today. This type of diverse education should not be simply available to all students, but compulsory.

I believe that to problem-solve modern day challenges heaped upon the old wounds of racism in our country, we must collectively acknowledge the treatment of abuse toward African Americans and other minorities. The only way to disrupt cycles of abuse is to study them as they are and implement changes which break these cycles. There will not be one solution, there will be many. But no solution can take hold without an acknowledgement of and reverence for the abuse as it is evidenced in our communities.

Finally, I believe that we must change our behavior toward, perspective of, and thinking about race in America. We are an adapting nation; we are a changing people. Americans today cannot afford to be a convert nation indifferent about police brutality or self-effacing about this malignant and perpetual issue of racism. If allowed, racism will harm education for all children, not just Black children. If allowed, racism will stunt all innovation, not just Black innovation. If allowed, racism will corrupt all systems of government, not just those which govern Black people. And if allowed, racism will hold all Americans back from reaching our true potential, not just Black Americans. We can change our understanding and perspective by listening to the experiences of others, learning from our past, and collaboratively mapping out an inclusive plan for our future. Abolishing racism — and with it, police brutality and other acts of systemic violence against minorities — may be the calling of this new generation of Americans.

Central High built a strong, impressive community of empathetic, committed alumni who are practiced in the art of building up others as they themselves rise. I have no doubt that if all Eagles joined forces, we could contribute to the growth of our local and national community in profound ways. And that, as they say, is the "Eagle Way."

Dr. Wead in 1971.

Photo courtesy of North Omaha History.

Dr. Rodney S. Wead is a recognized Civil Rights leader in North Omaha, and is known nationwide for his publications, teaching, and leadership for organizations in their outreach to minorities. He grew up in the Logan Fontenelle Public Housing Projects, and as a kid was a newsboy for the Omaha Star, a prominent local Black newspaper. He graduated from Central High School in 1953 and in 1957 earned a bachelor's degree from Dana College.

Dr. Wead began his prominent career in social services in Omaha. Starting in 1958, he worked at the Nebraska Psychiatric Institute as an educational therapist. Then in 1966, Wead became a VISTA program director for Catholic Social Action of Nebraska. In 1967, Dr. Wead became the executive director of the United Methodist Community Centers, and opened a new facility called the Wesley House. During his leadership there, Wead was instrumental in starting the Franklin Community Credit Union in 1968, the first bank in Omaha to offer loans to low-income constituents, and in 1970, he worked with native Omahans to establish the city's first Black-owned radio station, KOWH. He also established the Community Bank of Nebraska and the development of the Omaha Economics Development Corporation, which built a 200-unit housing center and a 10-unit strip shopping mall, as well as the nation's first 24-hour daycare center.

In 1976, he earned his master's degree from Roosevelt University in Chicago, and then earned his PhD in sociology at the Union Institute in Cincinnati in 1980. In 1983, Dr. Wead became the Executive Director of the United Methodist Community Centers, and later served as associate professor of Black Studies at University of Nebraska at Omaha and Creighton University. He was inducted into the first class of the Central High School Hall of Fame in 1999. Today, Dr. Wead lives in St. Louis, Missouri with his wife, Vanessa. In 2018, the Omaha City Council renamed a section of North 52nd Street "Rodney S. Wead Street" in honor of Dr. Wead.

This biography is courtesy of North Omaha History.

The Central High School Foundation is a 501 c(3) and was established in 1996 to provide support for present and future Central High School students. To ensure that the tradition of excellence continues, the Foundation supports the school through a variety of activities including alumni relations, fundraising, grant writing, student scholarships, capital projects, and teacher and classroom grants. With your support, the foundation can continue to honor the past, live successfully in the present, and plan for the future.

Click here: https://chsfomaha.org/support

ABOUT THE AUTHOR

This book is made possible because of my daughter, Dr. Ann Lineve "Nieve" Wead Kimbrough, who urged me to tell my story. She and I collaborated to produce our first book together. Nieve has been keeping notes on my life since she was about 10 years old. She kept a daily journal and was influenced to become a journalist by the late great Charles B. Washington, an Omaha Star newspaper columnist and my longtime friend. Also, the first black national journalist she was introduced to and who became her lifetime mentor, is Carole Carmichael. Carole was assigned to Omaha while working for United Press International wire service. Later, Carole arranged for one of my favorite authors, Toni Morrison, and I to meet prior to my introduction of Toni during a program in Chicago.

Nieve always had a close watch on me. She used to predict which airline flight would bring me back to Omaha after one of my international and domestic trips. My children often say I make them feel as if they are the "only child" since I spent and continue to spend quality time with them. With Nieve, we spent a lot of time together. When she was three years old, she became very sick and most of her beautiful black hair came out and we had it cut into a short afro – long before that was popular among young girls. Nieve also had sensitive skin and she could only use certain bath products and lotions. Later, while she was in high school in Chicago, I went with her to her dermatology appointments where she underwent special lamp treatments. Nieve always had patience for everyone. She did not talk much when she was little.

We remain close all these years. Nieve reminds me of my dear sister, Beverly Ann Wead Blackburn, who was very active and excelled in sports, academics and took care of so many young people at Horace Mann Junior High School. Beverly died in 1973 and our lives have never been the same. Yet, Nieve channeled her wit and will. She followed in her footsteps by becoming a member of Zeta Phi Beta Sorority, Inc.

Nieve likes to take great care of me. All my milestone birthday celebrations have been either organized or emceed by her. She can usually predict what I like and how I would like to see it presented.

Beyond this book, Nieve has plans for additional books, a podcast, virtual meetings, and other events that are largely involve new technology to communicate. Whether politics, history, or children, Nieve and I never tire of talking about just about every topic. She studied everyone and everything. It paid off in her years as a mother to three children, W. Earl, and twins John Charles and Jocelyn Cheryl. She powered through trying times with John Charles, who was born with an umbilical hernia that was followed by bacterial meningitis, infant seizures, loss of partial hearing and full loss of his eyesight.

Nieve never lost her vision to make sure that my life's story was published. I love her and appreciate everything that she has done to make sure the Wead family legacy is well documented.